HARMFUL ERROR

INVESTIGATING AMERICA'S LOCAL PROSECUTORS

"[The prosecutor] is the representative not of an ordinary party to a controversy, but of a sovereignty whose obligation to govern impartially is as compelling as its obligation to govern at all; and whose interest, therefore . . . is not that [he] shall win a case, but that justice shall be done . . . . He may prosecute with earnestness and vigor—indeed, he should do so. But, while he may strike hard blows, he is not at liberty to strike foul ones."

—Berger v. United States (1935)

HARMFUL ERROR

INVESTIGATING AMERICA'S LOCAL PROSECUTORS

A project of the
Center for Public Integrity

Summer 2003 Report

About the Center for Public Integrity

The CENTER FOR PUBLIC INTEGRITY, founded in 1989 by a group of concerned Americans, is a nonprofit, nonpartisan, tax-exempt educational organization created so that important national issues can be investigated and analyzed over a period of months without the normal time or space limitations. Since its inception, the Center has investigated and disseminated a wide array of information in more than a hundred Center Reports. The Center's books and studies are resources for journalists, academics, and the general public, with databases, backup files, government documents, and other information available as well.

The Center is funded by foundations, individuals, and revenue from the sale of publications. The project was funded by the Open Society Institute and The New York Community Trust-Everett Philanthropic Fund.

This report, and the views expressed herein, do not necessarily reflect the views of the individual members of the Center for Public Integrity's Board of Directors or Advisory Board.

THE CENTER FOR PUBLIC INTEGRITY
910 17th Street, N.W.
Seventh Floor
Washington, D.C. 20006
Telephone: (202) 466-1300
Facsimile: (202) 466-1101
E-mail: contact@publicintegrity.org
http://www.publicintegrity.org

ISBN: 1-882583-18-3

Printed in the United States of America

Team Members

Project manager
Steve Weinberg

Deputy project manager
Neil Gordon

Writer
Brooke Williams

Researchers
Caleb Gauen, L'Kenya Jackson, Kathleen Liu,
Julia Picard, Sara Towles, Rebecca Wein

Research Assistance
Augustin Armendariz, Ben Coates, Bob Fagen, Morgan Jindrich,
Daniel Lathrop, Alicia Oman, Katharine Widland

Executive director
Charles Lewis

Managing editor
Bill Allison

Deputy managing editor
Teo Furtado

Database editor
Aron Pilhofer

Research editor
Peter Smith

Web developer
Han Nguyen

Graphic artist
Jonathan Werve

IT Manager
Javed Khan

Table of Contents

Introduction

Since 1970, individual judges and appellate court panels cited prosecutorial misconduct as a factor when dismissing charges at trial, reversing convictions or reducing sentences in at least 2,012 cases, a three-year investigation by the Center for Public Integrity has found.

Sometimes the consequences are severe. In 28 cases, involving 32 separate defendants, misconduct by prosecutors led to the conviction of innocent individuals who were later exonerated, the Center found. Innocent men and women were convicted of serious charges, including murder, rape, kidnapping and assault.

Guilty defendants have also had their convictions overturned. Sometimes those defendants cannot be retried because of double jeopardy rules and are placed back on the streets of the community.

A team of 21 researchers, writers and editors analyzed 11,452 cases in which charges of prosecutorial misconduct were reviewed by appellate court judges. In the majority of cases, the allegation of misconduct was ruled harmless error or was not addressed by the appellate judges, and the conviction stood. Because of the relative rarity of reversals, any prosecutor who has more than one reversal to his or her credit belongs to a select club. These prosecutors give recidivism—a word usually used to describe those they work to put behind bars—a disturbing new meaning.

In Cuyahoga County, Ohio, Carmen Marino, who served for 30 years as a prosecutor before retiring in 2002, won five convictions that were overturned by the Ohio appellate courts. Appellate judges have ruled that Montgomery County, Ala., District Attorney Ellen Brooks' discriminatory tactics deprived defendants of fair trials four times since she began prosecuting in 1977. Former Hinds County, Miss., District Attorney Edward Peters was involved in six cases in which judges ruled that his conduct prejudiced a defendant.

Center researchers compiled state-by-state summaries, tracking misconduct across the nation:

• Of the 523 cases in which Pennsylvania defendants alleged misconduct, 287 were in Philadelphia. Judges reversed or remanded the conviction, sentence or indictment in 41 cases tried in the City of Brotherly Love.

- In 35 of the 120 North Carolina appeals which Center researchers studied, defendants pointed to Biblical references made by prosecutors as grounds for reversal.

- Appellate judges in Alabama cited discrimination in jury selection in 45 percent of the convictions they reversed.

- The Hennepin County District Attorney's office, which covers the Minneapolis area, was responsible for 88 of the 240 Minnesota criminal cases in which defendants alleged misconduct on appeal. In 12 of the cases, judges reversed or remanded the conviction, sentence or indictment because of the prosecutor's conduct.

The study also tracks the influence that the top prosecutor in a jurisdiction, elected in some, appointed in others, can have on an office. Since 1990—the year Walworth County, Wis., District Attorney Phillip Koss was elected to office—there have been at least 27 appellate decisions addressing alleged prosecutorial error. In the 20 years before that, there were three. In 12 of those 27 cases, judges ruled that the prosecutor's conduct required reversing the defendant's conviction.

In San Diego, the office of district attorney has been held by prosecutors who have attempted to make the office more accountable. Yet appellate judges ruled on allegations of prosecutorial error or misconduct allegations in 45 San Diego County cases, of which eight led to reversals, dismissals or acquittals. Of the 2,341 jurisdictions the Center researched, San Diego stood out for the attempts its top prosecutors made to do things differently. Perhaps a reflection of their success lies in the fact that the citizenry of San Diego County became so educated about prosecutorial misconduct that when it did occur, they were ready to hold the district attorney responsible and vote him out of office, no matter his accomplishments or intentions.

Front line prosecutors

In most jurisdictions, at least 95 percent of the cases that pour in from the police never reach a jury, which means any misconduct occurs away from public view. The only trial those defendants receive takes place in the prosecutor's office; the prosecutor becomes the judge and the jury. The prosecutor is the de facto law after an arrest, deciding whether to charge the suspect with committing a crime, what charge to file from a range of possibilities, whether to offer a pre-trial deal, and, if so, the terms of the deal.

The Center's investigation tracked career prosecutors, and found some who repeatedly broke the rules:

- The Wisconsin Court of Appeals has addressed Walworth County Assistant District Attorney Diane Resch's conduct at least ten times. In half of those appeals, judges ruled that her conduct warranted reversing the defendant's conviction. Three of those reversals, which included various constitutional violations, were child sex abuse cases.

- Missouri judges cited Nels C. Moss Jr., a St. Louis prosecutor, for misconduct in at least 24 cases, yet Moss never faced a disciplinary action during the more than three decades he has been a prosecutor. Over the course of his career, Moss failed to turn over potentially exculpatory evidence to the defense before trial; reneged during trial on a pre-trial stipulation with the defense; called the jury's attention to the defendant's failure to testify, thereby compromising the Fifth Amendment rights of the accused; alluded to the defendant's prior criminal record, a violation of the rules of evidence; attacked the character of the defendant with information not in the court record; used inadmissible material from a separate trial of an accomplice; promised during jury selection or opening argument to present testimony never offered; attacked the truthfulness of defense counsel; cast aspersions on the integrity of an insanity defense; and inflamed jurors' passions during closing argument.

- The repeated offenses of John Zimmermann, a Nashville prosecutor, led his colleagues, including former state attorneys general and U.S. attorneys, to document his misconduct in a brief submitted to the U.S. Supreme Court last year on behalf of a death row inmate, Abu-Ali Abdur'Rahman, whom Zimmermann had convicted.

Center researchers studied the conduct of local prosecutors, trying to understand their actions within the context of a very difficult job. They analyzed every accessible state appellate court opinion, trial court ruling and state bar disciplinary filing back to 1970 addressing allegations of prosecutorial misconduct. Researchers supplemented these findings with additional cases not reported in court records but available through media accounts or learned of through interviews and correspondence with journalists, inmates, defense lawyers, state bar disciplinary counsel, judges and other sources.

The case citations are available in a searchable, online database, along with summaries tracking misconduct in each of the 50 states.

Breaking the Rules
Who suffers when a prosecutor is cited for misconduct?

When Larry Johnson walked out of a Missouri prison during the summer of 2002, exonerated by DNA testing from a wrongful rape conviction after avowing his innocence for 18 years, St. Louis legal community insiders nodded knowingly as word trickled out who had led the prosecution back in 1984—Nels C. Moss Jr.

Moss, assistant circuit attorney for the city of St. Louis and later a trial prosecutor in neighboring St. Charles County, earned a well-deserved reputation as an aggressive, effective trial prosecutor. During his 33 years of trying cases for the people, however, he simultaneously was a recidivist breaker of the rules by which prosecutors are supposed to operate.

After joining the St. Louis city prosecutor's office in 1968, Moss found his conduct formally challenged in at least 24 cases. In seven of those, judges reversed the conviction, declared a mistrial or issued some other ruling adverse to the prosecution.

Over the course of his career as a prosecutor, Moss reneged during trial on a pretrial stipulation with the defense; called the jury's attention to the defendant's failure to testify, thereby compromising the Fifth Amendment rights of the accused; alluded to the defendant's uncharged criminal conduct, a violation of the rules of evidence; attacked the character of the defendant with information not in the court record; used inadmissible material from a separate trial of an accomplice; promised during jury selection or opening argument to present testimony never offered; attacked the truthfulness of defense counsel; cast aspersions on the integrity of an insanity defense; and inflamed jurors' passions during closing argument.

When one appellate panel reversed a conviction in a case won by Moss, a judge writing a concurring opinion emphasized that the blame lay with the prosecutor and not with the courts:

"Most regrettable ... is the fact that we are required to remand this case for retrial, with all of the expense, delay and inconvenience attendant thereto, because of a trial incident that need not and should not have occurred ... It was a deliberate effort by one of the most experienced assistant circuit attorneys in the City of St. Louis to interject even more poison than his extensive review of defendant's prior convictions had already accomplished ... The sole purpose ... was to poison the minds of the jurors regarding the defendant's character ... Where, as in this case, the record discloses a patent effort to deprive a defendant of a fair trial, the onus for the delay and added expense should be directed toward the prosecutor who caused it. This is especially true when, rather than resulting from youthful zeal, the error is but one example of a consistent pattern of improper tactics reflected by other transcripts in cases tried by the same experienced prosecutor."

In another 17 cases prosecuted by Moss, appellate judges affirmed the conviction or trial judges allowed the proceeding to continue, despite finding Moss committed prosecutorial error.

Moss declined an interview request from the Center for Public Integrity, and wrote that he sees no point in subjecting himself to "second guessing by those that have not walked in my shoes." In his response to the interview request, Moss characterized himself as "a hard-hitting but honest prosecutor." He estimated that he tried more than 400 cases before juries, including "high-profile, racially and politically explosive cases. Obviously the friends and representatives of those convicted are dissatisfied with the outcomes and are prone to see fault and perceived injustice."

Of judges who criticized his tactics, Moss wrote that some "have never tried cases as prosecutors or defense attorneys and have never experienced the heat of the courtroom." Moss wondered if his detractors realize that, "I have refused to proceed on numerous cases where confessions did not match the evidence, where identifications did not measure up to appropriate standards, where alibis while not conclusive have left too much reasonable doubt. ... I have never approved or sponsored testimony I suspected to be false. I have never prosecuted anyone on the basis of race; indeed most of the victims of the crimes I prosecuted were minorities."

Though Moss' record of 7 reversals due to misconduct and 17 other findings that he committed prosecutorial error is extreme, he is hardly an anomaly.

Recidivist prosecutors

Local prosecutors in many of the 2,341 jurisdictions across the nation have stretched, bent or broken rules while convicting defendants, the Center has found. Since 1970, individual judges and appellate court panels cited prosecutorial misconduct as a factor when dismissing charges at trial, reversing convictions or reducing sentences in at least 2,012 cases. The nature of the questionable conduct covers every type attributed to Moss, and more.

In 513 additional cases, appellate judges offered opinions—either dissents or concurrences—in which they found the prosecutorial misconduct serious enough to merit additional discussion; some of the dissenting judges wrote that they found the misconduct warranted a reversal. In thousands more cases, judges labeled prosecutorial behavior inappropriate, but allowed the trial to continue or upheld convictions using a doctrine called "harmless error."

The Center analyzed 11,452 cases in which charges of prosecutorial misconduct were reviewed by appellate court judges. In the majority of cases, the allegation of misconduct was ruled harmless error or was not addressed by the appellate judges, and the conviction stood. The relative rarity of reversals makes these opinions useful from an empirical standpoint: Any prosecutor who has more than one reversal to her credit belongs to a select club.

Prosecutorial misconduct falls into several categories, including:

• Courtroom misconduct (making inappropriate or inflammatory comments in the presence of the jury; introducing or attempting to introduce inadmissible, inappropriate or inflammatory evidence; mischaracterizing the evidence or the facts of the case to the court or jury; committing violations pertaining to the selection of the jury; or making improper closing arguments);

• Mishandling of physical evidence (hiding, destroying or tampering with evidence, case files or court records);

• Failing to disclose exculpatory evidence;

• Threatening, badgering or tampering with witnesses;

• Using false or misleading evidence;

• Harassing, displaying bias toward, or having a vendetta against the defendant or defendant's counsel (including *selective* or *vindictive prosecution*, which includes instances of denial of a speedy trial);

• Improper behavior during grand jury proceedings.

Some of the most common allegations of prosecutorial misconduct involved improper closing arguments and excluding jurors on the basis of race, ethnicity, gender or other discriminatory grounds.

In 28 cases, involving 32 separate defendants, misconduct by prosecutors led to the conviction of innocent individuals who were later exonerated, the Center found. Innocent men and women were convicted of serious charges, including murder, rape, kidnapping and assault.

Guilty defendants have also had their convictions overturned. Sometimes those defendants cannot be retried because of double jeopardy rules, and are placed back on the streets of the community. In other words, prosecutorial misconduct sometimes has severe consequences for the entire citizenry, not just a lone defendant.

In addition, the Center found some prosecutors who had convicted innocent defendants in more than one case over the course of their careers; some of these prosecutors were cited multiple times for misconduct in other cases as well.

Most of the nation's approximately 30,000 local trial prosecutors strive to balance their understandable desire to win—a desire supported by the vast majority of the citizenry—with their duty to ensure justice. There are some prosecutors, however, who have exalted winning and ignored the other half of the equation. Those prosecutors who repeatedly break the rules give *recidivism*—a word usually used to describe those they work to put behind bars—a disturbing new meaning.

It is impossible to know for sure how often a specific prosecutor (or a specific defense attorney, judge, police officer, etc.) bends or breaks the rules. In most jurisdictions, at least 95 percent of the cases that pour in from the police never reach a jury, which means any misconduct occurs away from public view. The only trial those defendants receive takes place in the prosecutor's office; the prosecutor becomes the judge and the jury. The prosecutor is the de facto law after an arrest, deciding whether to charge the suspect with committing a crime, what charge to file from a range of possibilities, whether to offer a pre-trial deal, and, if so, the terms of the deal.

Katherine Goldwasser, a law professor at Washington University in St. Louis who served as a prosecutor in Chicago before joining academia, suggested that misconduct often occurs out of sight, especially in cases that never go to trial. Those cases by definition do not generate appellate opinions (and thus are for the most part beyond the scope of the Center study). Goldwasser told the Center. "It is not a safe assumption that cases ending with guilty pleas are absent prosecutorial misconduct."

Perhaps the most difficult type of misconduct to unearth, Goldwasser said, is the failure of the prosecutor to turn over possibly exculpatory information to the defense. Such lack of disclosure is commonly known as a "Brady violation," after the 1963 U.S. Supreme Court case *Brady v. Maryland* and its progeny. After all, if only police and prosecutors know about evidence that suggests innocence, how is defense counsel to know for certain such evidence even exists?

To complicate quantification, any listing of mistrials and appellate reversals involving a specific prosecutor might be incomplete. While legal databases like Lexis and Westlaw (both of which were used in this study) contain appellate rulings, some remain unpublished, and those that are published rarely identify the trial prosecutor. And, short of visiting every courthouse in the country, there is no way to determine how many cases are dismissed or ruled mistrials by trial judges (and thus never reaching the appellate courts) because of a prosecutor's misconduct.

Despite those limitations in the data, the study determined that, like Moss in St. Louis, other prosecutors around the country have been found by appellate court or trial court judges to have bent or broken the rules multiple times.

In Cuyahoga County, Ohio, Carmen Marino, who served for 30 years as a prosecutor before retiring in 2002, won five convictions that were overturned by the Ohio appellate courts. Appellate judges have ruled that Montgomery County, Ala., District Attorney Ellen Brooks' discriminatory tactics deprived defendants of fair trials four times since she began prosecuting in 1977. Former Hinds County, Miss., District Attorney Edward Peters was involved in six cases in which judges ruled that his conduct prejudiced a defendant.

The pattern of behavior of John Zimmermann, a trial prosecutor in Davidson County (Nashville), Tenn., so alarmed six former Tennessee prosecutors that, during July 2002, they filed an *amici curiae* brief to the U.S. Supreme Court on behalf of Death Row defendant Abu-Ali Abdur'Rahman. The six, who constitute a who's who of the Tennessee legal profession, cited Zimmermann's misconduct in the case — confirmed by the state Supreme Court but nevertheless ruled as harmless error — and his behavior in previous, unrelated cases.

The brief argues that Zimmermann withheld evidence from the defense and misrepresented a prior conviction of the defendant. Even more troubling, it cites Zimmermann's conduct during three other, unrelated cases, including a murder case in which the verdict was overturned because of the Davidson County prosecutor's behavior. (In a response to the Center for Public Integrity, Zimmerman vociferously contests the charges.)

Fighting Misconduct

Perhaps nothing better demonstrates the serious problem prosecutorial error and misconduct pose to the justice system than the efforts of a handful of jurisdictions to combat it. In Boston, Ralph Costas Martin II, who became district attorney of Suffolk County in 1992, worked hard to change a system that had been characterized by one prominent defense attorney as "the best place to have a guilty client, and the worst one to have an innocent client," according to journalist Sean Flynn's book, *Boston D.A.: The Battle to Transform the American Justice System.*

Among numerous examples, Flynn explains how Martin began hiring young trial prosecutors who understood the concept of elevating justice over winning at all costs.

Job candidates would be asked how they would handle the following scenario: On a busy morning, with three dozen cases stacked up, you, the prosecutor, are approached by defense counsel in one of those cases. "My client will plead out if you recommend probation," the defense lawyer says. You skim the case file, which contains nothing but a police report. It says the officer stopped the car because the driver allegedly made a "furtive gesture." While searching the stopped car, the officer says he found a small amount of cocaine. What, the job candidate is asked, should a good prosecutor do?

The obvious answer seems to be accept the plea. But that is not the answer Martin wanted. Instead, he hoped job candidates would say they would ask the judge for a delay, in order to question the arresting officer privately. The first question of the officer should be to describe the "furtive gesture." Much of the time, Martin believed, police officers listed that rationale to cover up a bogus stop of a racial minority or some other targeted group. Unless the police officer offered a plausible explanation, Martin hoped the job candidate would say the case should be dismissed. Why? Because an alert defense lawyer or judge will understand the traffic stop was a pretext, thus leading to suppression of the evidence that resulted—the cocaine. The prosecutor moving ahead with the case will lose the trust of the judge and the defense lawyer, and will have done nothing to halt the police officer's improper behavior.

In San Diego County, elected District Attorney Paul J. Pfingst and his staff introduced a number of innovations, including distribution of a comprehensive training manual to all attorneys in the office, initiation of post-conviction DNA review of 766 pre-1992 cases, and even allowing television cameras to follow prosecutors around as they did their work. The videotape became the basis of a national television show that aired weekly on NBC during the summer of 2002. But not even all the legitimate reforms could save Pfingst from defeat at the polls in November 2002. Too many voters perceived his office as housing prosecutors whose misbehavior resulted in high-profile mistrials and appellate reversals.

Within a jurisdiction, elected prosecutors can preside over a culture of misconduct in their offices. Unelected, nearly anonymous prosecutors, like Nels Moss in St. Louis, do not operate in a vacuum. Individual prosecutors accused of misconduct must be understood within the context of the culture of the office to which that prosecutor belongs.

The St. Louis Circuit Attorney's office has served as a home for aggressive trial prosecutors, including Moss. Sometimes that aggressiveness leads to brilliant lawyering within bounds. Other times it leads to rule breaking.

Since 1970, the Center study found, there were 129 rulings by trial judges and appellate judges, including the cases tried by Moss, that addressed alleged prosecutorial error by the circuit attorney's office.

Those cases involve at least 40 St. Louis city prosecutors other than Moss. Of the 129 rulings, 45 resulted in reversals or acquittals. Another 13 upheld convictions, but at least one appellate judge issued a dissent in favor of reversing the conviction. The remaining 71 rulings found prosecutorial error, but the judges allowed the convictions to stand, without any dissents.

A culture of misconduct

Bennett L. Gershman, a former New York County (Manhattan) prosecutor who now teaches law at Pace University, is an authority on professional conduct. Gershman, who has written textbooks and law review articles about prosecutorial misconduct, testified at Congressional hearings, conducted seminars and provided perspective to countless journalists, told the Center about St. Louis, "Compared to other offices that I have looked at, the number of reversed cases for prosecutorial misconduct from a single office is rather large, particularly since reversals are not commonplace given the various techniques used by appellate courts to try to uphold convictions."

Moss is not the only prosecutor in the St. Louis office to be cited multiple times for error and misconduct. Three assistant circuit attorneys other than Moss were cited or reversed multiple times for misconduct. Appellate judges cited misconduct when reversing three convictions won by Joseph W. Warzycki, who joined the circuit attorney's office in 1977. In five other cases, defendants alleged misconduct, which was ruled as harmless error. Gordon L. Ankney, now in private practice, was reversed twice for misconduct. John D. Chancellor was reversed once for misconduct; in 13 other cases, defendants alleged misconduct but appellate courts ruled it harmless error. Chancellor left the prosecutor's office in 1987 to become a trial judge, a position he held until his death in 1991.

Though St. Louis-area defense lawyers mention Warzycki, Ankney, Chancellor and other prosecutors from time to time, Nels Moss almost always is mentioned first, and discussed with the greatest amount of passion. Like so many other prosecutors who bend or break the rules in jurisdictions across the nation, Moss has never been publicly sanctioned by his office supervisors or by the state bar disciplinary counsel.

Gershman, the Pace University professor, said of Moss' record that the number of "reversed cases from one prosecutor's misconduct is fairly astounding."

Ronald Weich, a former assistant district attorney in New York County (Manhattan), has studied the atmosphere of prosecutors' offices and the conduct of individual prosecutors in those offices from his perch at the Washington, D.C., law firm of Zuckerman Spaeder. The co-author of a study for the Leadership Conference on Civil Rights that addresses what he terms "the unequal treatment of minorities in the exercise of prosecutorial discretion," he told the Center that, "Prosecutorial abuses often arise from structural problems and an utter lack of accountability within the office." When the elected prosecutor cares little about serving justice, that attitude trickles down to the trial prosecutors, Weich says. Even when the elected prosecutor sets the right tone, Weich believes many offices house what he calls "cowboys" who ignore reasonable doubt. Moss's career in St. Louis suggests that both office culture and his own aggressiveness played a part in his "astounding" record of reversals due to misconduct.

Moss served 16 of his 33 years as a prosecutor under the supervision of former Circuit Attorney George A. Peach, the elected district attorney. Peach, who first won election in 1976, resigned in 1992 because of personal financial and sexual improprieties. A staff prosecutor before his election to the top spot, Peach is one of the more than 40 prosecutors whose conduct led to reversals and other findings of error.

Dee Joyce-Hayes and Moss worked as trial prosecutors from 1981 until 1992 under Circuit Attorney Peach. Both Joyce-Hayes and Moss wanted to succeed Peach after he stepped aside in 1992. Joyce-Hayes won the job.

Joyce-Hayes told the Center she thought of firing Moss, partly because she believed he behaved unfairly toward her as a political opponent, partly because of his overaggressiveness as a trial lawyer. She retained Moss, she said, to keep from angering some of their office colleagues, to refrain from alienating certain St. Louis power brokers who admired Moss—and because he could win convictions that might have eluded other prosecutors. But, Joyce-Hayes added, "I isolated him in the homicide unit; I did not make him a team leader. I worried about him having too much contact with impressionable young assistant circuit attorneys."

The current elected prosecutor in St. Louis is Jennifer M. Joyce, who joined the staff before Moss left but never served as his supervisor. Joyce, who has served about half of her first four-year term, has instituted a number of reforms aimed at cleaning up the office culture of St. Louis.

Though Moss' elected supervisors failed to discipline or rein him in, he was ultimately responsible for his own conduct in the courtroom. And that conduct earned him the mistrust of lawyers who opposed him at trial. Some defense attorneys began to assume that Moss would bend or break rules.

During 1999, shortly after he left his position in St. Louis to prosecute cases in neighboring St. Charles County, Mo., Moss entered a high-profile murder case. Appellate courts had overturned the defendant's death sentence two separate times before his involvement.

Upon Moss' entry, public defenders collaborated on a petition they said was unprecedented in their experience: They asked the judge to bar Moss' participation.

Failing that, they asked the judge, before the proceeding even began, to admonish Moss "against engaging in any effort to circumvent the constitution ... the rules of evidence, and from any effort to make prejudicial arguments, speaking objections or other improper remarks within the hearing of the jury." The public defenders told the judge they had "no desire to engage in vexatious bickering, yet Mr. Moss comes to this case with a record of deliberate misconduct that sharply jeopardizes defendant's right to and hope for a fair, constitutional sentencing hearing."

The judge allowed Moss to enter the case. The trial got off to a bad start, as defense counsel had feared. The public defender complained to the judge that "Yesterday morning before we began opening statements, we ... received from the prosecuting attorney, Nels Moss, an endorsement of four new witnesses and then a number of items, a photo album. ... The matters that have now been disclosed are brand new witnesses, documents, items that have not previously been disclosed. ... We are at a significant disadvantage." The judge did not grant a mistrial. Moss eventually argued in favor of the death penalty, which the jury granted him.

Defense counsel appealed, alleging improper conduct by Moss. The Missouri Supreme Court agreed that, once again, Moss had conducted himself improperly. The court, however, upheld the death sentence, ruling Moss' overall performance, despite some specific "improper" conduct, could not be proved to have prejudiced the jurors:

"The three trials of this case unfortunately exhibit a consistent attempt by the prosecutor to push the envelope of proper advocacy. We condone the prosecutor's strategy no more in this trial than in the previous two that were reversed."

Judges scolded Moss in others cases, too, where they nevertheless upheld the conviction under a doctrine called "harmless error." Prosecutors and defense counsel disagree on the term's meaning. The former tend to emphasize the word "harmless," while the latter tend to stress the word "error."

Moss' partisans note that appellate judges—those with no trial experience, those with criminal defense backgrounds and even those who once served as prosecutors—sometimes misinterpret the antiseptic written trial record from which they work. As a result, appellate judges might find prosecutorial misconduct where none was intended. Those same partisans emphasize that Moss helped convict hundreds of guilty defendants without allegations of improper conduct arising on appeal.

Convicting the innocent

There is no doubt, however, that in cases like Larry Johnson's, unambiguously innocent defendants suffer for a long time while the perpetrators remain at liberty.

Determining unintentional error or intentional misconduct by the prosecution in an actual innocence case can be difficult; sometimes the prosecutor has sound reason to believe in the suspect's guilt until new evidence, or new ways to evaluate old evidence, emerge. The justice system is acknowledged by all its participants to be imperfect, and even when there is no misconduct, when there are no lapses—either intentional or unintentional—on the part of the police, the prosecutor, the judge, or the defense counsel, an innocent defendant can go to prison. At virtually any step in a trial, from the initial questioning of a suspect through the marshalling of forensic evidence and experts to closing arguments and appellate maneuvering, errors by the state—prosecutors and police—can convict the innocent.

In the Johnson case, Moss had plenty of reason at first to think the defendant guilty, given the accused rapist's criminal past and the victim's eyewitness identification. It is also worth noting that DNA testing, which eventually cleared Johnson, was not easily available nor particularly credible when the case first came to trial.

The rape that led to Johnson's arrest occurred Jan. 31, 1984. The next day, the victim helped a police artist produce a composite drawing of her assailant. He appeared clean-shaven, based on the victim's recollection. With the composite completed, the police artist showed the victim about 140 photographs of possible suspects. The victim set one of those photographs aside. The man pictured wore a mustache, contradicting the victim's original description. Moss asked the police artist to add a mustache to the composite. The artist complied.

Later that day, the victim picked Johnson from a police line-up. He had facial hair, contradicting the original physical description and the original composite.

When Johnson's public defender asked the victim questions at a deposition in late June, she said she was "fairly certain" the photograph she chose from the 140 looked like her assailant. During the August trial, a police crime analyst said he found sperm, but said nothing about using it to type the perpetrator's blood. Defense counsel asked about blood typing. Moss objected, and the judge sustained the objection. Why? Because the judge opposed allowing forensic tests into evidence.

As a result of Moss' objection and the judge's ruling in Moss' favor, the jurors convicted Johnson based solely on eyewitness testimony. He lost his only appeal, limited to jury selection issues, in 1986. So Johnson remained in prison, with no realistic hope of a hearing to reconsider his conviction, until 1995, when a letter he wrote to the Innocence Project staff in New York City meshed with their interest in post-conviction DNA testing.

Lawyer Barry Scheck, director of the Innocence Project, sued the St. Louis prosecutor's office toward the end of Dee Joyce-Hayes' term. Current prosecutor Jennifer Joyce inherited the litigation.

The Innocence Project staff claimed the prosecutor's office was obstructing post-conviction DNA testing in at least six rape cases, including Johnson's. Joyce responded there had never been obstruction. She said testing is being done, as time and budget permit, in accordance with a new Missouri law and U.S. Justice Department guidelines. Scheck and his staff are failing to consider the anguish of rape victims when cases are re-opened, Joyce said, as well as ignoring the common-sense theorem that testing should occur only if the results can definitively establish innocence or guilt. Since the litigation began, Joyce took the initiative to start examining about 1400 pre-1994 convictions, to determine if DNA evidence exists and, if so, whether it makes sense to test it. Joyce estimated each case will require about 10 hours of initial review after the paperwork is gathered.

The first scientific testing related to the Innocence Project litigation, on behalf of convicted rapist Fred Hamilton, confirmed his guilt. The finding cast a shadow over Scheck's effort and led St. Louis prosecutors to complain about wasting time and money, as well as forcing Joyce's staff to, as she put it, "re-victimize the victim" by asking her about sexual relations with men other than the rapist. "It was a gut-wrenching interview," Joyce said. "It reminded me of my time as a sex-crimes prosecutor." She wondered whether Hamilton believed he might benefit from a testing mistake, or whether he was acting sadistically.

Then the tables turned. The second DNA test, negotiated in court on behalf of Johnson, demonstrated a wrongful conviction. After spending 18 years behind bars for a crime he did not commit, Larry Johnson finally attained his freedom. And a long-standing miscarriage of justice was finally undone.

Anatomy of Misconduct
There's much to learn when a trial goes terribly wrong

On January 2, 1983, in the early morning hours, James A. Buckley died at a service station in St. Louis County. The 19-year-old white male attendant had been shot seven times, with robbery as the apparent motive.

When 24-year-old Ellen Reasonover heard about the murder on the television news later that day, she mentioned to her mother that she had stopped at the service station after midnight to seek change for the laundromat. As she approached the cashier's cage, Reasonover recalled, she saw a black male inside, walking to the rear of the building. She assumed he was the attendant, but he didn't respond to her knocking. Reasonover glimpsed two other black males in the shadows of the service station lot, but thought nothing of it. She then drove to a nearby convenience store for the change she still needed.

Reasonover's mother urged her to contact the police, who'd asked the community for tips that might help solve the homicide. Ellen Reasonover did as her mother suggested. When she called the police, she used a made-up name, but used her true name as soon as she arrived at the police station.

When police asked Reasonover why she had used a false name over the telephone, she explained that, as a black woman dealing with detectives under pressure to solve a murder with a young white male victim, she had to overcome a lifetime of generalized distrust. Furthermore, her half-brothers were criminals known to local police, causing Reasonover concern about guilt by association. But she understood her civic duty, she said, so she decided to come forward.

Imagine Ellen Reasonover's surprise when, later that year, a jury convicted her of Buckley's murder. Sixteen years later, a federal judge—a Republican appointee who had once served as a prosecutor—released Reasonover from prison. Reasonover, the judge concluded, was almost certainly innocent, and without question had been a victim of prosecutorial misconduct.

Steven Goldman, the prosecutor who put Reasonover in prison and whose misconduct, the federal judge ruled, contributed to the miscarriage of justice, benefited from the high-profile conviction; the voters of St. Louis County elected him to a state court judgeship.

Reasonover's case shows what can go wrong as prosecutors collaborate year in, year out with the same group of police officers, forensic scientists, expert witnesses and judges. They come to trust each other, developing bonds that sometimes lead to short-cuts. If the evidence is weak, it becomes easier to ignore those weaknesses or paper them over. At each step, errors are ratified rather than exposed.

What follows is a catalog of lessons about prosecutors and their allies in the criminal justice system, revolving around an intensive study of Reasonover's conviction. Though her case is extreme, the kinds of misconduct that occurred can be found in hundreds of other cases.

Lesson One: Premature conclusions can ensnare the innocent. Police detectives assumed Reasonover's guilt within a few days of the murder, seeming to disregard evidence that pointed away from her, according to available documents. Prosecutor Goldman apparently adopted those assumptions in preparing his case against Reasonover.

Police asked Reasonover to view mug shots of possible perpetrators. They told her not to worry about a perfect match. Rather, police told her to look for features similar to the men she reported glimpsing from a distance in the shadows of the service station. When Reasonover identified pictures of two men who turned out to be incarcerated for other offenses, police arrived at the conclusion that she must be trying to deflect suspicion from herself. They put Reasonover in a jail cell, with no access to a lawyer. By contrast, when another potential witness, a white male, pointed to one of the same mug shots that Reasonover had chosen, the police did not put him in a cell.

Within a couple of days, the prosecution team allowed Reasonover to leave jail without filing charges against her. But, according to available documents, it appears investigators were so fixated on Reasonover that they did little to pursue other leads, such as service station visitors who reportedly had purchased marijuana from the victim at work; an individual with whom the victim fought at a party the month before; and area robbers with a modus operandi similar to what occurred the night of the murder.

Lesson Two: Lack of solid evidence does not prevent charges from being filed. Charging a suspect despite lacking physical evidence (no weapon, no blood, no saliva, no semen, no skin, no hair); no reliable eyewitness testimony; no credible confession; no clear motive; and no coherent theory of the crime is often a bad move. Police and prosecutors lacked all those elements in the case of Ellen Reasonover. Before the arrest, authorities possessed no hint of Reasonover's involvement other than their reaction to her perceived behavior after she voluntarily called the police with information.

A prosecutor's authority to charge someone with a crime is an awesome power, without any realistic, meaningful checks. Conscientious prosecutors understand the danger. New York City prosecutor Mark D. Cohen states it plainly: Charges should not be filed to use as leverage in plea bargaining, or to enhance a prosecutor's political standing, he says. Other prosecutors may use the National District Attorneys Association standards, which make clear that charges should be filed only if they "can be substantiated by admissible evidence at trial." Some elected district attorneys have tried to limit abuse by making the decisions themselves in questionable cases.

In Brooklyn, N.Y., elected district attorney Charles Hynes told his staff prosecutors that he would personally decide whether to charge a suspect based on a single eyewitness account. Hynes instituted the policy because Brooklyn had for several years suffered embarrassment due to wrongful convictions. He says that during a recent yearlong stretch, he rejected 15 of 70 proposed prosecutions because the sole eyewitness in the rejected cases lacked credibility.

Of course, when the elected prosecutor or a deputy district attorney makes the final decision there's always the danger that pressures related to electoral politics will play a role. E. Michael McCann, the elected prosecutor in Milwaukee, Wis., since 1968, has stood for re-election several times and understands the temptations. "The discretion of the district attorney is broad and subject to almost no control or judicial review," McCann said. "The burden of proving that a district attorney has abused his or her discretion ... because of political ambition or community pressure will be extremely difficult, if not impossible, to prove." Take for example a prosecutor who files a charge in a weak but sensitive case, figuring "a closing argument artfully orchestrated to stoke the passions of the jury but not so fevered as to trigger reversal will surely tempt those jurors to convict, overriding doubts that ought to persist due to deficiencies in the evidence. In such cases, only the district attorney will know what the defense attorney, the judge and the investigating officers may suspect, and the jury never perceives: that the district attorney has compromised the precious integrity of his or her office."

Whether prosecutors are seeking higher office or not, McCann worries about how many never reduce or dismiss a charge as new evidence becomes available. Too many prosecutors have a mistaken notion that the original decision is "garbed with a pristine quality, and any reduction therefrom appears to cast the district attorney in an adverse light and to compromise the integrity of the criminal justice system. ... In some cases, an elected district attorney, not wishing to reach a politically unpalatable but proper decision, justifies inaction by saying, 'Let the jury decide.' While this may appear to be graced with a patina of deference to the jury system, it is in fact an abdication of the district attorney's responsibilities. The jury will rarely, if ever, know as much about the case as the prosecutor."

Lesson Three: Prosecutors can tilt the system of checks and balances. Theoretically, a grand jury of citizens called from the registered voter rolls serves as a check on a prosecutor. So should the judge at the preliminary hearing. In practice, grand juries and judges rarely serve as a brake on prosecutors. But the system of checks and balances can fail, as it did in the Reasonover case. A grand jury heard the prosecutor's evidence and indicted an innocent woman.

Traditionally, grand juries hear only the prosecution's case, and the anecdotal evidence is overwhelming that grand juries hardly ever fail to follow the prosecutor's lead. Mark Cohen of New York says that in many jurisdictions his colleagues have no obligation to tell grand juries about exculpatory or mitigating evidence. Such behavior is almost never discussed publicly. Journalists have no access to grand juries. Grand jurors themselves are supposed to remain silent. Defendants and their lawyers worry that they will be unable to negotiate with prosecutors later if they make grand jury proceedings the battleground for allegations of state error or misconduct.

Still, there are appellate court rulings that shed light on how a prosecutor can improperly manipulate a grand jury. A New Jersey ruling, for example, threw out the sexual assault indictment of James H. Gaughran in Hudson County (Jersey City). The victim, a 17-year-old woman, made the allegations against the 19-year-old Gaughran, whom she'd known for about nine months. The alleged assault occurred during an evening of smoking marijuana and drinking beer. Gaughran maintained that they'd had consensual sex. An examination of the woman at a hospital emergency room tended to support his version. Here is what the grand jurors heard about the medical examination:

Question by the prosecutor: "And were you taken to the Jersey City Medical Center?" Answer: "Yes, I was." Question: "And were you given a gynecological exam while you were there?" Answer: "Yes."

In overturning the conviction, the appellate court commented: "The results of the exam were not given to the grand jurors. They were not given the defendant's statement. Nor were they advised of the drug use by the victim ... The defendant contends the medical examination directly supports the defendant's version and directly contradicts the victim's version. The state concedes the report is exculpatory but argues it has no duty to present exculpatory evidence."

The appellate judges in the Gaughran case made it clear they disagreed with the state's contention. "It is essential that the jurors be informed of the relevant facts," they wrote. "The evidential impact of the medical report should not be underestimated. It directly contradicts the victim's claim of anal and vaginal penetration and does not support her claim of a one and a half hour struggle. The Grand Jurors could not have been expected to ask for the results of the medical exam. They were skillfully misled by omission into believing it had corroborated the victim's testimony. By withholding relevant and highly exculpatory evidence in its possession, the State treated this Grand Jury as a rubber stamp, its playtoy, and clearly infringed upon this Grand Jury's decision-making function. In fact, given the nature of the medical report and its devastating impact on the presentation, the failure to present it can be termed an intentional subversion of the process."

Another "subversive" tactic prosecutors may use at the grand jury stage involves what is referred to as "saving back" one or more charges arising from the conduct leading to trial. If something goes wrong for the prosecution, those withheld criminal charges might be used to pressure the defendant into accepting a plea bargain. Saved back charges are supposed to be barred from future prosecution if known to the district attorney at the time of the original prosecution.

At the preliminary hearing stage, a judge can serve as a check on a prosecutor. Again, however, the anecdotal evidence is abundant that few weak cases are thrown out at preliminary hearings. Individual prosecutors see the same judges over and over, day after day. Banter can turn into professional friendships and sometimes social friendships. Ex parte communications, without defense counsel present, might start to seem normal.

Robert N. Kepple of the Texas District and County Attorneys Association said it might unfold like this: "The court has a lot of cases set on the docket Monday. The judge is a former prosecutor, the type who still asks the prosecutor 'Are we ready?' The judge, over coffee before the docket call, asks you about the cases set for trial that day. You know that what the judge wants to do is evaluate the one...he feels is worth trying." Kepple says the ethical prosecutor has a simple solution available—common sense: "The key to avoiding problems with ex parte communications is to remember the very definition of ex parte, that is, a communication [involving] fewer than all of the people legally entitled to participate. If prosecutors are always mindful of who should be or would want to be involved in a communication, they can avoid trouble."

Lesson Four: Prosecutors should cautiously evaluate testimony and confessions. Police and prosecutors in various jurisdictions place too much value on apparent confessions, jailhouse informants and eyewitness testimony. Confessions sometimes turn out to be wrong, be it because they were coerced, the suspect was mentally ill, or the suspect confessed after a jailhouse informant concocted a story about hearing an admission of guilt. Eyewitness testimony may also turn out to be wrong: DNA evidence has shown that even a rape victim in the closest proximity imaginable to the perpetrator has misidentified the attacker. In the Reasonover case, authorities lacked a confession, eyewitness testimony, physical evidence or motive—raising serious questions about the decision to charge her. They did, however, have the testimony of two jailhouse informants.

Goldman made deals with two inmates who briefly shared the same cell with Reasonover at different times. Both inmates suffered from prior credibility problems; both told stories of alleged Reasonover confessions that violated common sense; both received future considerations from Goldman that were never disclosed to the defense or the jury. Years later, when Reasonover was represented by highly competent, persistent lawyers, one of the two informants refused to repeat her allegations under oath. The other could not be interviewed again because she had committed suicide.

Reasonover supposedly confessed spontaneously to an inmate named Rose Jolliff. Another inmate in the same cell, Marquita Butler, despite being pressured to confirm Jolliff's account, told police and prosecutors that Jolliff was lying. Jolliff had not worn a recording device; the prosecution team possessed only her verbal account, which both Butler and Reasonover denied.

Five days later, after Reasonover had been released from police custody, the prosecution team arranged for Jolliff to call their suspect, hoping to entrap Reasonover. During the conversation, Reasonover mentioned her innocence eight times—to the same woman who supposedly heard an unprovoked confession five days earlier. Reasonover and her trial lawyers never knew about the recording of that conversation, which suggested innocence, before facing the jury that voted for a murder conviction.

The confidence prosecutors place on informants is surprising given how easy it is for an experienced convict to manipulate the system. Problem confessions, informants and eyewitness testimony have backfired again and again. But the learning curve is either temporary or non-existent in numerous jurisdictions. Confessions sometimes turn out to be false, maybe because of coercion by the interrogators, maybe because of the suspect's mental illness, maybe because a jailhouse informant concocted a story about hearing an admission of guilt. The informants rarely provide information without expecting a payoff. As for eyewitness testimony by informants, victims or bystanders, it is sometimes filled with error for all sorts of well-intended or nefarious reasons.

Milwaukee District Attorney E. Michael McCann says that decades of working closely with police have led him to comprehend the false confessions phenomenon. The veteran prosecutor learns the degree of rectitude demonstrated by each officer, the biases of some. "The prosecutor may see the officers interrogate prisoners and hear their testimony, as well as that of the interrogated prisoners, during motions to suppress confessions. This experience can materially aid the conscientious prosecutor in a hard-nosed assessment as to whether police overreaching was involved in securing a confession and how much reliance should be placed on inculpatory statements reported but challenged by the accused. However, while long-term working relationships with officers can provide significant information as to their credibility or suspected mendacity, such contacts can also give rise to friendships that may impair the prosecutor's capacity for critical assessments of claims of police overreaching in security confessions...Other prosecutors, being of unconscionably timorous bent, may be unwilling to confront police hostility occasionally triggered by a decision not to use a confession with the adverse implications that such a determination has for a conviction."

McCann says that while a confession might not be out-and-out fabricated by police, it might still be untrue because of the suspect's mental instability combined in some way with the tactics used to extract the confession. He worries about lack of candor by police "critical to the jury's determination as to how trustworthy the confessions are." Based on his experience, McCann says "On occasion, either in response to the district attorney's question or by a volunteered comment, an officer or commander of integrity will tell the district attorney that he or she has doubts about the veracity of a confession."

More and more courts are allowing the defense to present expert testimony about the prevalence of false confessions, including the reasons behind the surprisingly large numbers. In such circumstances, prosecutors often labor mightily to discredit the defense expert. That is no surprise—the testimony should be scrutinized in front of a jury because the generalizations might be inapplicable to the particular case.

Just as more and more courts are allowing defense experts to testify about the false confession phenomenon, more and more courts are allowing defense experts to explain why eyewitness testimony is sometimes unreliable. The eyewitness testimony used by prosecutors sometimes turns out to be well intentioned but mistaken, sometimes intentionally misleading. Police who question eyewitnesses can exercise a huge influence. McCann in Milwaukee worries about the "overzealous officer who inappropriately suggests information to a witness and who pushes an identification witness for more certainty than the witness has. Some officers carefully record both inculpatory and exculpatory information. Other officers tend to brush aside exculpatory statements and record principally inculpatory ones."

DNA evidence is beginning to persuade previously strong advocates of relying on confessions and eyewitness testimony that they are mistaken more frequently than the conventional wisdom has allowed. When DNA testing demonstrates that even a rape victim in point-blank proximity to the perpetrator misidentified the attacker, all eyewitness testimony must be evaluated with care.

The pervasiveness of prosecutors using informants, and informants using prosecutors, came to the attention of many laypeople in 1989, in large part because the *Los Angeles Times* outed professional informant Leslie Vernon White. Reporters Ted Rohrlich and Robert W. Stewart opened their expose like this:

"When veteran jailhouse informant Leslie Vernon White picked up a telephone last fall and showed authorities how easily he could fake the confession of another inmate, he cracked open a window on a secret world. At any given time, Los Angeles County jails hold between 50 and 100 informants—many of them career criminals like White— who have engaged in relentless campaigns to implicate their fellow prisoners in crimes, and thus earn the ultimate favor from authorities: early release from custody."

Before the White expose, prosecutors repeated their mantra to journalists, defense attorneys and other skeptics over and over: Yes, informants can be risky to use. But we have a two-pronged test we apply. Did the informant tell us details known only to the criminal? And did the informant and the defendant spend time together in jail?

White demonstrated that the two-pronged test could be compromised. As the *Times* reporters explained, "Equipped with only a telephone and the last name of the inmate he did not know, White impersonated police officers and prosecutors and squeezed enough information from law enforcement officials to fabricate a plausible confession. Then he created a phony record showing that he and the accused had been together in jail."

The *Times* reporters studied "dozens of criminal cases involving alleged inmate confessions." Three involved confessions faked by inmates and used against other suspects. In "many other" cases, the *Times* reporters could not tell for sure whether inmates had lied about confessions by others. Furthermore, threats by police and prosecutors that jailhouse informants would testify if a case proceeded to trial caused defendants to plead guilty in exchange for reduced sentences. The *Times* reporters determined that when defendants did go to trial, the prosecution had used jailhouse informants on the witness stand in hundreds of cases. Although it is usually impossible to prove what goes through a prosecutor's mind, the *Times* reporters found credible evidence that at least some Los Angeles County prosecutors knew their jailhouse informants were lying, but called them as witnesses anyway.

Lesson Five: Prosecutors should not rely uncritically on their scientific and forensic experts. Reasonover was given a stress test—a modified lie detector test—which was ruled inadmissible in court. A prosecution witness was hypnotized to recover a memory of what he'd seen on the night of the murder. His hypnosis-induced recollection and subsequent testimony implicating Reasonover's boyfriend was allowed to stand.

When understood and used properly, forensic and other technological evidence can be powerful tools. But the evidentiary value of such forensic material can be diminished when it is mishandled, improperly labeled, or poorly inventoried by police officers. Sometimes, even when the evidence is collected properly, the analysis may be faulty or the forensic scientist untrustworthy. Fred S. Zain in West Virginia and Joyce Gilchrist in

Oklahoma City are among the forensic technicians employed by police departments who are best-known for their alleged incompetence or their willingness to doctor evidence.

Zain is known to have provided misleading evidence in numerous trials that helped the prosecution and hurt the defense. It is unknown whether prosecutors using his evidence knew about the problems; it is known, however, that even after Zain came under suspicion, some West Virginia prosecutors continued to ask that he specifically conduct forensic tests because they disliked the results from other scientists.

Zain, a law enforcement officer, began directing the serology division of the West Virginia State Police Crime Laboratory in 1979. Some of his staff suspected his competence and honesty at an early stage, but either said nothing or had their suspicions ignored by police superiors. All that began to change in 1987, with the trial of Glen Dale Woodall for assault. As one of the prosecution's experts, Zain testified that his scientific examination of semen recovered from the victims matched Woodall's blood type. Statistically, Zain testified, the chance of such a match was six in 10,000.

Appellate judges upheld the conviction. But Woodall and his lawyers refused to give up, and in a habeas corpus proceeding they convinced the state Supreme Court to order DNA testing. The results proved Woodall's innocence. The trial court freed him from prison five years into his maximum 335-year term. Woodall sued for damages. The state's insurer began an investigation that included a review of Zain's work. The findings led to a $1 million payment for Woodall.

A subsequent investigation into Zain's work led to a West Virginia Supreme Court ruling that all convictions involving Zain's findings would be analyzed to determine if the remaining evidence supported those convictions. The state Supreme Court commented that the details of Zain's conduct "are shocking, and represent egregious violations of the right of a defendant to a fair trial. They stain our judicial system and mock the ideal of justice under law." The judges directed Kanawha County prosecutor William C. Forbes and the U.S. attorney to determine whether Zain should be charged with a crime.

A Kanawha County grand jury indicted Zain in 1998 for providing false testimony in the prosecutions of James E. Richardson, John Earl McLaurin and Jimmy C. Gardner. At Zain's trial, jurors could not reach a unanimous verdict; Zain died of cancer at age 52 in December 2002, before he could be retried. At the time of his death, a dozen prisoners had been released or scheduled for retrial because of his testimony; the state had paid at least $6.5 million in damages to inmates.

While Zain was being prosecuted, an August 2001 ruling by the U.S. Court of Appeals for the Tenth Circuit in the case of Alfred Brian Mitchell was casting serious doubt on the work of Oklahoma City forensics expert Joyce Gilchrist. The case wended its way to the federal circuit after an Oklahoma City trial court found Mitchell guilty of murdering a college student volunteering at a community center for disadvantaged juveniles during 1991. The court also found Mitchell guilty of rape and sodomy.

The conviction and death sentence rested partly on the testimony of Gilchrist, a forensic chemist with the Oklahoma City Police Department. Gilchrist's testimony about her examination of the physical evidence, coupled with other testimony that the victim and her boyfriend last had sexual relations eight days before the murder, convicted Mitchell.

Before trial, Gilchrist sent the evidence to Michael Vick at the Federal Bureau of Investigation laboratory's DNA unit for testing. At trial, Gilchrist characterized Vick's report as inconclusive. It was much later, during an evidentiary proceeding supervised by a federal judge as part of Mitchell's appeals, that the defense saw Gilchrist's notes of her conversations with Vick. Those notes suggested that the FBI's tests cleared Mitchell of committing rape either before or after murdering the victim. One of Gilchrist's own tests had the same result.

In reversing the death penalty, the Tenth Circuit judges commented not only on Gilchrist, but also on the trial prosecutor: Gilchrist "provided the jury with evidence implicating Mr. Mitchell in the sexual assault of the victim which she knew was rendered false ... by evidence withheld from the defense. Compounding this improper conduct was that of the prosecutor, whom the [federal] district court found had 'labored extensively at trial to obscure the true DNA test results and to highlight Gilchrist's test results,' and whose characterization of the FBI report in his closing argument was 'entirely unsupported by evidence and ... misleading.'"

Not all questionable forensic evidence stems from lies, tied to pro-prosecution bias. So-called expert witnesses sometimes have weak credentials, or rely on hokum posing as science. Prosecutors around the nation used to retain the services of a University of North Carolina-Greensboro anthropology professor named Louise Robbins, who said she could match crime-scene footprints to the footwear of perpetrators. Few other forensic scientists endorsed the validity of Robbins' techniques. But prosecutors called on Robbins over and over, banking on the good will of the trial judge to certify her as an expert. Robbins helped convict defendants across the nation until her technique was shown to yield results that were no better than chance would have produced.

Robbins probably would have remained below the radar of most defense lawyers, legal scholars, journalists and general readers except for her involvement in an especially egregious case of prosecutorial zealotry. The case began in 1983, with the abduction of a 10-year-old girl from her comfortable home in DuPage County, part of the Chicago suburbs. When searchers found her body two days later, they saw she had been assaulted and murdered. Finally, more than a year later, prosecutors—under pressure from the girl's parents, elected officials and the citizenry at large—charged three men based on very questionable evidence. About a year after the arrests of Rolando Cruz, Alejandro Hernandez and Stephen Buckley, the trial began. Jurors found Cruz and Hernandez guilty, but deadlocked on Buckley. By the end of 1985, a career criminal named Brian Dugan had confessed to murdering the girl, acting by himself. He passed a lie detector test, and convinced numerous observers, including seasoned law enforcement officers, that he indeed abducted and murdered the victim. The prosecutors and the trial judge refused to believe Dugan, however. So Cruz and Hernandez sat on death row while their appeals proceeded. Buckley, meanwhile, wondered whether and when prosecutors would re-try him, based largely on Robbins' testimony about his shoes.

Chicago Sun-Times reporter Thomas Frisbie watched the case unfold. Like other observers, he thought Robbins' testimony against Buckley violated common sense, not to mention scientific principles. So he started contacting other anthropologists and forensic scientists in related fields. Every scientist Frisbie contacted demeaned her work. Robbins herself would not discuss the validity of her techniques in the Buckley case with Frisbie. A law professor who taught a course on scientific evidence told Frisbie it seemed the only standard used by prosecutors and judges allowing Robbins to testify as an expert "is that it be incriminating to the defendant."

DuPage County State's Attorney Jim Ryan finally announced during early 1987 that his office would not re-try Buckley, in large part because Robbins was suffering from a serious illness. "Apparently," Frisbie said, "Ryan could find no other expert who would support Robbins' conclusions." Robbins died later that year. Eventually, both Hernandez and Cruz would also be cleared.

The next year, an Illinois appellate court reversed the murder and sexual assault conviction of Dennis J. Ferguson. Robbins had been a prosecution witness. The appellate judges ordered a new trial for Ferguson largely because of their finding that Robbins' testimony was worthless. The judges added, however, that the prosecutor aggravated the situation by frequently misstating the evidence. The prosecutor iced that impermissible behavior with this passage from the closing argument: "You have to believe that they [prosecution witnesses] are all liars or fools, every one of them. And for you to find the defendant not guilty ... you have to believe he told you the truth. You have to feel his brothers told you the truth. And that all of the persons I just named are liars and fools. It is your decision." The appellate judges noted "For a prosecutor to inform a jury that in order to believe the defense witnesses the jury must find that each of the State's witnesses was lying is such a misstatement of law as to prejudice the defendant and deny him a fair trial."

Lesson Six: Some prosecutors still withhold evidence. In Ellen Reasonover's case, prosecutor Goldman withheld a tape recording suggesting her innocence, a recording made without Reasonover's knowledge while she was in a jail cell. It is possible that police gave it to him without commenting on its contents. But it is unlikely that Goldman never listened to the tape, especially given his reputation for thoroughness. The tape captures a 56-minute conversation between Reasonover and her former boyfriend as they sat in separate, nearby holding cells secretly rigged by police with recording devices. Police and prosecutors suspected the former boyfriend of collaborating with Reasonover and another man to murder the service station attendant. The tape captures two people sounding befuddled about why they are in jail, about why they are suspects. The conversation by itself does not prove innocence, but if introduced at trial could have pushed one or more jurors into the realm of reasonable doubt.

The recording came into evidence during a post-conviction proceeding because of a private investigator's question to a prosecution witness many years after trial. At that point, the state could have professed ignorance, could have claimed the tape had been destroyed, or otherwise frustrated Reasonover's post-conviction lawyers. Fortunately for Reasonover, a prosecutor other than Goldman, upon request, looked for the recording, located it, and provided it to Reasonover's last-ditch appellate lawyers. Without it, Reasonover would still be serving her prison term.

Most prosecutors do not destroy evidence that could establish innocence. It does happen, though, and probably more often than prosecutors themselves acknowledge publicly. For example, while compiling a primer on prosecutorial behavior in Kentucky, defense lawyer Jerry J. Cox found multiple appellate rulings revolving around destruction of evidence.

Withholding evidence that might be favorable to the defendant is called a Brady violation, after a 1963 U.S. Supreme Court decision. That ruling involved a 1958 homicide in Anne Arundel County, Md., that demonstrated the ugly consequences of non-disclosure.

John Leo Brady, a 25-year-old abandoned by his parents while a baby, a poor student, an Air Force enlistee with a spotty record leading to premature discharge, an indifferent employee drifting from menial job to menial job, found himself broke while his girlfriend was pregnant. When he noticed the new car of a long-time acquaintance, physically slight, hard-working loner William Brooks, age 53, Brady decided to steal the Ford Fairlane. Brady planned the theft with Donald Boblit, the developmentally disabled brother of his girlfriend. The available evidence suggests that Brady had no intention of killing Brooks, who had treated him generously in the past. But, that same evidence suggests, Boblit panicked during the car theft, beating Brooks and then strangling him to death. After their arrests, Brady and Boblit told conflicting stories. Among his various versions, Boblit told authorities that he, not Brady, was responsible for the homicide.

Prosecutor C. Osborne Duvall apparently never considered telling Brady's defense lawyer about that confession, nor did Duvall have to do so by law. Brady and Boblit both ended up on Death Row. A prison chaplain who believed Brady's account that Brooks died at the hands of Boblit convinced E. Clinton Bamberger Jr., a former Catholic school student of his, to consider helping with an appeal. Bamberger, a former prosecutor with the state attorney general's office, had come to believe in a level playing field while working for the government.

Bamberger obtained the transcripts from the separate trials of Brady and Boblit. The Brady trial transcript yielded no grounds for appeal. But in the Boblit transcript, the lawyer noticed a vague reference to a July 9, 1958, confession, called the "fifth statement." Examining the exhibits attached to the transcript, Bamberger found four statements, but not the July 9 document. When he obtained that document, which included Boblit's confession, he used it as the basis for Brady's appeal.

A Maryland court accepted the appeal, and, later, so did the U.S. Supreme Court. Writing for the majority, Justice William O. Douglas stated, "the suppression by the prosecution of evidence favorable to an accused upon request violates due process where the evidence is material either to guilt or to punishment, irrespective of the good faith or bad faith of the prosecution ... Society wins not only when the guilty are convicted but when criminal trials are fair; our system of the administration of justice suffers when any accused is treated unfairly."

It might seem simplest for prosecutors automatically to provide everything—except the identities of confidential informants—in their files to the defense. Some prosecutors indeed operate like that. Some do not; it is human nature to want to win, and turning over everything sometimes makes obtaining a conviction more difficult.

The gray areas can be immense. The timing of the disclosure is one of those gray areas. If a prosecutor hangs onto Brady material long enough, it might lose its value for the defense. For example, if the prosecutor delays disclosure of significant evidence with exculpatory or impeachment potential, the defendant will be disadvantaged before the trial when deciding whether to accept a plea agreement rather than risk an uncertain fate in front of a jury.

Douglas R. Roth, a Sedgwick County (Wichita), Kan., prosecutor, instructs his colleagues in a chapter of *The Prosecutor's Deskbook* to "avoid the temptation of making a self-determination that the possible exculpatory evidence is not credible or admissible and therefore does not need to be disclosed to the defense. The test under Brady is not whether the evidence is admissible. ...Given a prosecutor's duty to seek the truth and to not convict innocent persons, the firm belief that a particular defendant is guilty should always be subject to reasonable review and re-evaluation."

Admonitions such as Roth's seem to be ignored more frequently than previously thought. "For a while after the Brady decision, every occurrence of withholding by a prosecutor meant a risk for the prosecution," Katherine Goldwasser, a former federal prosecutor in Chicago who now teaches law at Washington University in St. Louis, told the Center. Her first boss taught her "If it hurts, turn it over to the defense." Law and practice have moved a long way from that maxim, Goldwasser says, as courts have provided prosecutors new loopholes. To demonstrate a Brady violation today, the defense must prove non-disclosure of normally secret information, then demonstrate that the non-disclosure contributed to a guilty verdict.

"Legal standards will never stop diabolical prosecutors," Goldwasser said. "But going back to the original Brady standard could stop a basically decent prosecutor from withholding information useful to the defense. Most prosecutors aren't out to break the rules."

Many prosecutors emphasize that turning over everything is simplest. Joshua Marquis, the elected district attorney in Clatsop County, Ore., says it is his policy: "I say give the defense everything. What's the downside, as long as you don't jeopardize an informant's life? It's an easy call for me." A few prosecutors mentioned that sometimes the discovery material helps defense attorneys see their clients' lies, making a plea bargain easier to reach.

Lesson Seven: A pattern of excluding potential jurors by race or gender should raise a warning. A jury of all whites tried Reasonover, despite a substantial minority population in St. Louis County. The use of peremptory challenges by the prosecution (or the defense) to remove a certain type of juror from the panel might be grounded in impermissible racism or sexism.

Proving a violation, however, is usually impossible, absent a leaked smoking-gun memo or an obvious historical pattern, because it requires reading the mind of the prosecutor. If the prosecutor can offer a reason for each challenge that sounds race-neutral or gender-neutral, there is nothing a trial judge or appellate judges can do but nod their heads.

Defense attorneys talk about extreme instances where they believe the prosecutor dropped the criminal charges in the middle of jury selection because of an unfavorable looking panel, only to refile the charges later in hopes of drawing a more favorable panel.

Just as racial or gender bias continues to be an issue for American society at large, the fairness of jury selection will likely be questioned in some cases. During 2002, the *Dallas Morning News* demonstrated the continuing nature of the problem with a front-page story containing this opening paragraph: "A Supreme Court ruling in the case of Texas death row inmate Thomas Miller-El, convicted of killing an Irving hotel clerk, could set a standard for proving racial discrimination by prosecutors in jury selection, legal experts say." The defendant's lawyers first raised the jury fairness issue during the 1986 trial. The trial judge found no evidence of wrongdoing, but the appellate process kept the allegations alive until the U.S. Supreme Court agreed to hear oral arguments in October 2002.

In an eight-to-one decision, the U.S. Supreme Court said Miller-El should receive a substantive hearing from a lower court on his allegations about jury selection. The court majority said, "A comparative analysis of the venire members demonstrates that African-Americans were excluded from [Miller-El's] jury in a ratio significantly higher than Caucasians were. Of the 108 possible jurors reviewed by the prosecution and defense, 20 were African-American. Nine of them were excused for cause or by agreement of [both] parties. Of the 11 African-American jurors remaining, however, all but one were excluded by peremptory strikes exercised by the prosecutors. On this basis, 91 percent of the eligible black jurors were removed by peremptory strikes. In contrast, the prosecutors used their peremptory strikes against just 13 percent (four out of 31) of the eligible non-black prospective jurors qualified to serve ... " Furthermore, the court majority ruled, during the questioning of potential jurors, prosecutors used different tactics based on race when asking about willingness to invoke the death penalty.

Such conduct at trial, combined with persuasive evidence about the Dallas County District Attorney's office's historical practice of discriminating against African-American potential jurors, led to the court majority's lopsided vote in Miller-El's favor.

Lesson Eight: Juries empowered to impose the death penalty might be more likely to convict. Anecdotal evidence and social science research suggest that excluding all potential jurors who oppose the death penalty changes the tenor of deliberations. It is apparently human nature to think that when the death penalty is on the table, the defendant must be guilty, or the prosecutor would request a lesser punishment. Reasonover faced a jury who could impose the death penalty. After the jurors found her guilty, 11 of the 12 voted to execute her, despite a case based solely on police suspicions and the testimony of two jailhouse informants. Only one juror stood between Reasonover's death at the hands of the state and her later release from prison by a federal judge.

In the Dallas case of Miller-El heard by the U.S. Supreme Court, his lawyers argued that the prosecution used peremptory challenges to eliminate 10 of 11 possible black jurors while retaining whites with similar backgrounds. The state claimed that the blacks stricken through peremptory challenges expressed unwillingness to impose the death penalty, which meant their exclusion from the jury would be justified by law. "The vast majority of non-minority panelists favored the death penalty and were willing to impose it, while the majority of African-American panelists were opposed to the death penalty or unwilling to impose it," the state's brief argued. Some supporters of Miller-El's position argued that the state's line of reasoning promotes unfairness because it suggests that African-Americans in general are less desirable as jurors than whites because of differing views about imposing a death sentence. Miller-El's petition referred to a *Dallas Morning News* series based on 100 randomly selected felony trials. It showed that 86 percent of blacks eligible for jury duty ended up not serving because of prosecutors' peremptory challenges.

Lesson Nine: Improper opening statements and closing arguments and direct and cross-examinations can infect the fairness of a trial. An appellate court in the Reasonover case said the prosecutor "was consistently blatant in his use of leading questions" posed to the jailhouse informants during trial. But because Reasonover's trial lawyers never objected to the leading nature of the questions, the appellate court would do nothing about the problem.

Defense lawyers are generally vocal about prosecutors' conduct during trials—that is part of their job, after all. But sometimes judges, from the bench, issue some of the strongest condemnations of prosecutorial tactics.

Paul E. Pfeifer, an Ohio Supreme Court justice, explained in a commentary article his dissent in an appeal from death row inhabitant Angelo Fears: "A prosecutor's 'overzealous' remarks may not seem that important. After all, why should prosecutors restrain themselves when all they are doing is trying to convict a guilty person? In fact, it is extremely important. Our system of justice is ... founded on the principle that no matter how guilty a defendant may appear, the accused shall receive an impartial trial; everyone according to the same rules. But in this case, Angelo Fears' prosecutors time and again made statements during the trial that may have unfairly influenced the jury. For example, the prosecutors defamed a psychologist who testified as an expert witness. The prosecutors called the doctor the 'mouth piece' of the defense, insinuating that the defense paid the expert simply to have him parrot their opinions. The prosecutors also made repeated references to notes that the doctor took during an interview with Fears. The judge had already ruled that the state couldn't view the notes, but the prosecutors kept bringing them up, making it appear to the jury that important information was hidden in those notes." Pfeifer warned that if prosecutors in the Fears case and other cases "don't reign themselves in, a guilty criminal will wriggle out of a conviction because of prosecutorial misconduct."

In North Carolina, the state Supreme Court lectured prosecutors on improper closings in an opinion that vacated a death sentence: "The issue of improper closing arguments has become a mainstay, if not a troublesome refrain, in cases before this court. In virtually every capital case, many other criminal cases, and a growing number of civil cases, this issue is being vigorously advocated as grounds for reversible error. Therefore, we take this opportunity to revisit in some detail the limits of proper closing argument; the professional and ethical responsibility of attorneys making such arguments; the duty of our trial judges to be diligent in overseeing closing arguments; and the possible ramifications for failing to keep such arguments in line with existing law." The court added, "If attorneys were to scrupulously comply with these seemingly simple requirements, then the issue of alleging improper argument on appeal would prove an exception instead of the rule. Regrettably, such has not been the case; in fact, it appears to this court that some attorneys intentionally 'push the envelope' with their jury arguments in the belief that there will be no consequences for doing so."

Amie L. Clifford, assistant director of the National College of District Attorneys, warns her colleagues about the types of misconduct that can occur during closing arguments, such as commenting about the defendant's failure to testify at trial; characterizing prosecution evidence as uncontradicted when the only person able to contradict it with certainty is the defendant, who chose not to testify; making direct statements about the defendant's refusal to participate in a post-arrest interview with law enforcement officers; issuing derogatory comments about the defendant that could be considered name calling ("animal," "monster," "pervert," etc.); injecting personal opinion in a manner that amounts to vouching for a witness ("I submit to you that I think the victim is telling the truth about the details of the rape, despite the lack of semen."); appealing to the jury's prejudices or passions, such as comparing the heinous nature of the crime at issue to the Columbine High School mass murder; stating to the jury that an acquittal will lead to dire consequences for the community, such as heightened gang crime sprees; asserting personal knowledge concerning facts not in evidence.

Defense lawyers Daniel E. Monnat of Wichita and Paige A. Nichols of Lawrence, Kan., have identified 10 kinds of prosecutorial misconduct during closing arguments. The first five fall under their label "elementary misconduct": referring to facts not in evidence; commenting about the defendant's failure to testify or present evidence; name calling or scare tactics meant to inflame jurors; begging for sympathy, such as asking jurors to place themselves in the victim's shoes; and stating personal opinions, including bolstering the credibility of state's witnesses as well as impugning the credibility of the defendant, defense counsel or defense witnesses.

The next two fall under the label "distorting the burden of proof": arguing that the jury cannot acquit unless it finds state's witnesses are mistaken or lying; and arguing that the jury must convict if it finds the defendant or defense witnesses lied. Next is "denigrating defense tactics": suggesting that the defense theory of the case is a sham.

Finally, come two points under the label "misstating the jury's responsibility": minimizing jurors' obligations by suggesting appellate courts can correct mistakes; and overstating jurors' obligations by asking them to support law enforcement or send a message to the criminal element.

Prosecutors, in various professional publications, show they are aware of the closing argument and cross-examination pitfalls. Jean G. Sturtridge, a St. Clair County, Mich., prosecutor, advises colleagues that the state "should not use the power of cross-examination to discredit or undermine a witness if the prosecutor knows the witness is testifying truthfully." Another precept: Prosecutors "should not ask a question that implies the existence of a fact that he either knows to be untrue or has no reasonable, objective basis for believing is true."

Al M. Dominguez, the elected prosecutor for Colorado's 19th District, based in Greeley, admonishes colleagues to stay away from all kinds of tricks during cross-examination, including some that might be legal. Dominguez singled out a technique called "pitting." "During direct examination, the defendant testifies to a story that totally contradicts ... prosecution witnesses," he wrote. "During cross-examination, the prosecutor asks the defendant whether all the other witnesses are lying. ... Because testimonial inconsistencies between witnesses can be the product of mistake or another cause, it is misleading and unfair to give the jury the impression that the witness is lying. It is the province of the jury to weigh the credibility of the witnesses ... "

Lesson Ten: Prosecutors should not interfere with defense access to prosecution witnesses or tamper with witnesses for either side. In the Reasonover case, defense counsel experienced difficulties trying to talk to the two jailhouse informants before trial.

Douglas R. Roth, writing in *The Prosecutor's Deskbook*, warns his colleagues to refrain from obstructing defense access to witnesses. "The best practice for prosecutors is to instruct witnesses, preferably in writing, that they may talk with defense representatives if they choose to but that they are not obligated to."

Misconduct can also occur when a prosecutor needs to contact a defense witness. "Just visiting a defense witness and interviewing [him] does not raise ethical concerns," says Robert N. Kepple of the Texas District and County Attorneys Association. "But just how far can a prosecutor go when it comes to telling the witness [he or she] is less than impressed with the story? The key may be intimidation. Did the prosecutor act in a way that intimidated a witness into not testifying?" If the question ends up before a judge, the issue usually revolves around allegations that a prosecutor threatened a witness with perjury. "A prosecutor cannot engage in deliberate and badgering threats designed to quash significant testimony," he adds. Prosecutors are also limited in what they can say to those testifying for the state. If a witness contradicts an earlier account, the prosecutor can warn the witness to be truthful, but cannot emphasize such warnings to the point that intimidation seems to be involved. A refusal to grant immunity from prosecution for the prior inconsistent testimony can be a form of intimidation, in that it is meant to bind the witness to one particular version, whether true or not. Even when the state's witness is credible at first and remains consistent in her account, there is what Kepple calls "a balancing act that prosecutors must perform every time they prepare a witness for trial." That balancing act allows detailed discussion of the law and the facts, as well as the importance of certain facts. But untruthfulness or even shading the facts to fit a particular scenario cannot be encouraged.

Former prosecutor Bennett L. Gershman is pessimistic that witness-coaching can be monitored, given the private settings in which it occurs. Calling witness-coaching the "dark secret" of prosecutorial conduct, Gershman says wrongful convictions and other documented errors of the criminal justice system can often be linked to "techniques used by prosecutors to prepare, shape and polish the testimony of their witnesses." Based on his own experience as a prosecutor as well as his research since becoming a law professor, Gershman says it is "indisputable that some prosecutors coach witnesses with the deliberate objective of promoting false or misleading testimony. Prosecutors do this primarily to eliminate inconsistencies between a witness's earlier statements and her present testimony; avoid details that might embarrass the witness and weaken her testimony; and conceal information that might reveal ... the prosecutor has suppressed evidence."

Lesson Eleven: Appellate courts sometimes ignore exculpatory evidence withheld due to misconduct. The year after Reasonover's murder conviction, a team of *Washington Post* reporters began investigating the conduct of police and prosecutors, based on a tip. The Post story referred briefly to the secretly recorded jailhouse conversation between Reasonover and her former boyfriend, but the reporters did not know the precise contents of the tape. Reasonover's first team of appellate lawyers requested the tape, but the state replied that the two individuals "did not discuss anything of substance concerning the killing," adding that the prosecution "should not be faulted for not disclosing a conversation which contained nothing of evidentiary value to either party."

In other words, the state cast doubt on Reasonover's credibility because she never discussed details of a murder she said she never committed. The appellate judges neither asked for nor heard the tape. In their denial of Reasonover's original appeal, the judges said: "Although it would appear that [the tape] should have been disclosed to the defense, absence of any indication in the record of the content of the conversation prevents our determination of whether the state's failure in this regard amounts to prosecutorial misconduct warranting reversal."

The appellate judges also brushed aside the prosecution's failure to fully disclose deals with the two jailhouse informants, because, the judges said, they could not decipher the criminal-history printouts of the informants, so chose not to bother with that evidence.

It's not uncommon for appellate judges to give prosecutors a pass, excusing their missteps with the term "harmless error." If a prosecutor bends or breaks a rule, even if the violation appears to be intentional, appellate judges can say they fail to see how a change in conduct would have altered the verdict. It is the equivalent of the vernacular "No harm, no foul." Most of the time, appellate judges refuse even to identify the offending prosecutor by name.

"The harmless error rule, once an appellate mechanism to prevent technical violations from upsetting a verdict, has evolved into the most powerful judicial weapon to preserve convictions despite serious errors or misconduct," Gershman writes. "And whereas habeas corpus historically was invoked to vindicate fundamental constitutional rights, the Great Writ has been rendered almost nugatory by procedural obstacles to the bringing of claims and by increased deference to state court interpretations of federal constitutional guarantees."

Former Kansas prosecutor and trial judge Robert L. Gernon agrees, as he views allegations of misconduct from his perch on the appellate bench. Back in 1967, Gernon notes, U.S. Supreme Court Justice Potter Stewart recognized the quandary of a harmless error rule, saying it committed the court "to a case-by-case examination to determine the extent to which we think unconstitutional comment on a defendant's failure to testify influenced the outcome of a particular trial. This burdensome obligation is one that we here are hardly qualified to discharge."

Gernon said the contradiction is inherent: "Appellate courts will not reweigh the evidence. However, at times that is precisely what reliance on the harmless error rule requires." The inherent contradictions result "in a sliding-scale approach to some cases. The exact same conduct will result in a reversal if the case is close, but an affirmance if the evidence of guilt is strong."

With habeas corpus relief from the federal courts severely restricted by a 1996 Congressional act, sound appellate decisions by state courts are more vital than ever to the functioning of the criminal justice system. Reasonover's habeas petition made it to the federal courts just before the new law mandated a cutoff. As Barry Scheck, Peter Neufeld and Jim Dwyer write in their book, the Antiterrorism and Effective Death Penalty Act of 1996 closed a relief valve. The law "gives condemned prisoners six months after their state appeals to ask for federal intervention, and sets a one-year time limit for all other cases."

Lesson Twelve: Individuals from outside the criminal justice system are often the only post-conviction hope of those denied a fair hearing. Judges do not often revisit closed cases, relying on the concepts of harmless error and finality. Defense attorneys may not care, or they may be overwhelmed with other cases, or they may not be competent enough to investigate. In Reasonover's case, an investigation by the tiny, not-for-profit Centurion Ministries of Princeton, N.J., followed by Centurion's hiring of post-conviction lawyers from Kansas City, Mo., made the difference.

Other outsiders made a difference on Reasonover's behalf. On Christmas Day 1998, for example, a private investigator who had helped on an early Reasonover appeal saw an article in the *St. Louis Post-Dispatch* about the convicted murderer's attempt to clear her name. The investigator called one of Reasonover's last-ditch appellate lawyers, offering to turn over his old files. In those files, the lawyer noticed evidence of a previously undisclosed leniency deal between the prosecutor and one of the jailhouse informants. The information appeared in a memo from the informant's public defender to an office colleague. The memo said the informant "is going to be a witness in a capital murder case that Steve Goldman is trying ... After she testifies, she is going to plead guilty [to a charge unrelated to Reasonover] ... and be given probation. The details of the plea can be worked [out] after she testifies. The state does not want to allow ... defense attorneys to bring up any kind of deal that might have been made ... I have been assured by Steve Goldman that the state isn't going to burn her, that she will receive probation."

Lesson Thirteen: Police and prosecutors sometimes do little to search for the actual perpetrators of a crime after learning the original suspect is innocent. Although police and prosecutors in the Reasonover case said they had identified her two alleged accomplices, they never charged either man with murder. Furthermore, when the Centurion Ministries investigation identified a plausible murderer, St. Louis County authorities did nothing, at least publicly. With Reasonover freed, the killing of the service station attendant remains unpunished and unsolved. As many as three murderers might be at liberty to kill again. But as far as police and prosecutors are concerned, they cleared the case from the books.

.

A Question of Integrity

Prosecutors dispute the significance of 'prosecutorial misconduct'

After a recent Delaware Supreme Court decision, Wilmington lawyer Charles M. Oberly III wrote to E. Norman Veasey, the chief justice. Oberly, a veteran prosecutor now in private practice, had something to get off his chest about the court's ruling on another prosecutor's case. A lower court had granted the defendant a new trial partly because of "prosecutorial misconduct," a term repeated by the state's highest court in its ruling.

"The clear connotation of the word 'misconduct' is purposeful misbehavior," Oberly wrote. "During my 25 years being associated with the criminal justice system, I do not recall any instances in which a prosecutor intentionally caused error or behaved in a manner to cause a reversal of a conviction. The terminology is both unfair and demoralizing. If a defense attorney errs, the court simply refers to it as ineffective assistance of counsel or some other less damaging word. If the court errs, the judge is not designated as having committed 'misconduct.' I would like to respectfully request that the court cease using the word 'misconduct' unless the peculiar circumstances clearly call for such terminology. Instead, I would suggest that errors committed by the prosecution leading to a reversal and a new trial simply be referred to as prosecutorial error."

In the next paragraph, Oberly added a personal reference: "Approximately 20 years ago, a case of mine was reversed and the words 'prosecutorial misconduct' were used. I have never forgotten the feeling that the opinion implied—that I intended to do something wrong."

The chief justice sent a reply, addressed to "Dear Charlie."

"Although we understand your concern about the use of a term that includes the word 'misconduct,' it has become a term of art. A Westlaw search from 1944 to date reflects that the term 'prosecutorial misconduct' has been used by state courts 12,672 times, district courts 2,302 times, circuit courts 4,470 times and the United States Supreme Court 58 times. ... In the Dorsey case, we simply quoted the trial court's use of that term. As you know, the trial judge was Richard Gebelein, the former attorney general. ... We believe it would be confusing to change the terminology in view of this history."

Oberly is not the only prosecutor, former or current, to object to the word "misconduct." In a new book called *The Prosecutors Deskbook: Ethical Issues and Emerging Roles for 21st Century Prosecutors,* written by prosecutors for prosecutors, the following paragraph appears on the first page of the preface:

"Prosecutors often must face misperceptions and negative images of their activities communicated through the media. For example, allegations of 'prosecutorial misconduct' too often surface as defense trial tactics that are superficially aired in the popular media. In truth, allegations of 'prosecutorial misconduct' are rarely substantiated and are confused with occasional 'prosecutorial error' which does not involve professional misconduct."

That view is echoed by the National District Attorneys Association, the professional group that represents prosecutors, in the organization's magazine, *The Prosecutor*: "Frequently, a defendant, in an effort to find any basis for appeal, will claim prosecutorial misconduct produced his conviction rather than a fair and impartial trial," staff member Paula Wulff wrote in the July-August 2002 issue. "In most instances, these charges are dismissed by the reviewing court as groundless. Occasionally, however, the court's evaluation of the prosecutor's conduct is deemed to have created substantial prejudice such that the defendant was denied due process. In rare instances, a finding of prosecutorial misconduct has risen to a level where reversal is considered the proper outcome."

In another recent book by and for prosecutors, *Doing Justice: A Prosecutor's Guide to Ethics and Civil Liability,* James E. Punch Jr., an assistant district attorney from Sedgwick County (Wichita), Kan., noted that misconduct claims "seem to be increasing almost exponentially in recent years," making it "a given" that many cases will involve prosecutorial misconduct allegations from defense counsel. "It is almost impossible to read the reported cases from any jurisdiction and not find cases where prosecutorial misconduct is alleged or even has been found by the court to have occurred." Rather than despair at the unfairness of it all, Punch advised prosecutors to be prepared to respond to the allegations quickly and effectively. "A prosecutor must know in advance the law concerning claims of misconduct. It is now simply another part of trial preparation."

That means prosecutors must know not only how to deal with what they consider to be ill-motivated misconduct claims, Punch wrote; they must also know themselves. "Many of us have that moment in trial when we realize that we have acted inappropriately. Perhaps an objection was lodged that calls the action to our attention. Or we come to the realization on our own after some time for reflection. However a prosecutor learns that a mistake has been made, it is vital that a prosecutor act promptly and forthrightly. The worst thing is to do nothing and hope that no one discovers what happened. Cover-ups are almost always exposed. If it is discovered that the prosecutor knew of the inappropriate action and did nothing, it is almost guaranteed that not only might the conviction be reversed, but also the prosecutor may be facing lawyer discipline. In addition to those penalties, the prosecutor's reputation in the legal community will be damaged in a way that may be irreparable. It is much better to be known as someone who admits to ... errors than someone who tries to hide them."

"Even if defense counsel has acted improperly," Puntch adds, "this does not give you a license to respond in kind. Draw the court's attention to the objectionable conduct and request the proper relief. Do not respond in kind. The rules for prosecutors and defense counsel are vastly different. That may not seem fair, but it is a fact."

Roderick W. Leonard, a Los Angeles County deputy district attorney, explains: "An attorney's most valuable asset is not trial ability; it is the attorney's reputation. Think of attorneys who are not trusted. Lack of trust invariably results from actual or perceived violation of professional ethics ... Relations with that attorney become formal ... of necessity ... in writing or in court and on the record. A prudent attorney who must litigate against a lawyer of questionable legal ethics is advised to seek pretrial judicial orders to protect against possible unethical conduct. ...Motions ... and protective orders against the attorney's possible improper conduct during trial may become the norm ... How effective is an attorney, civil or criminal, defense attorney or prosecutor, who has a reputation for questionable ethical integrity?"

Punishing the Wrongfully Convicted

Federal law keeps defendants denied a fair trial—
including those who may be innocent—behind bars

The cliché about American jurisprudence is that the system is designed to let 10 guilty men go so that the proverbial one innocent man does not end up behind bars. By and large, the system does work that way. Prosecutors must prove their case beyond a reasonable doubt. Defendants do enjoy constitutional rights to defense counsel, to not incriminate themselves and to be free of searches unless the police show probable cause.

Yet a 1996 law has undermined the central protection of the accused—the right of habeas corpus, which the Founders considered so important that they included it in the Constitution even before the Bill of Rights was proposed—so severely that defendants convicted in unfair trials remain in prison, even some who appear to be innocent of the crime charged.

Habeas corpus (Latin for "you have the body") is a writ designed to release a prisoner from an unlawful imprisonment. A prisoner must file a petition for a writ of habeas corpus, which directs the detaining authority—normally a prison warden—to bring the prisoner to court for a determination of the legality of his or her imprisonment and whether or not he or she should be released from custody. The "great writ" is guaranteed by Article I of the U.S. Constitution and by state constitutions.

Law enforcement officials across the nation pushed Congress and President Bill Clinton to enact what eventually became known as the Antiterrorism and Effective Death Penalty Act. The new law's intent was to bring finality to the criminal justice process by limiting habeas petitions filed by inmates after they have been convicted. In addition to setting time limits during which a habeas petition can be filed, the law requires federal courts to defer to state court rulings, unless the rulings are shown to be clearly unreasonable.

The provisions of the 1996 law might prevent the release from prison of Darryl Burton, convicted of a 1984 St. Louis murder he most likely did not commit.

Burton's defense lawyers suspected police and prosecutorial misconduct early on, given the lack of physical evidence and a plea bargain with an alleged eyewitness named

Claudex Simmons, who was already charged with a felony in an unrelated case. In the beginning stages of the case, not even Burton's lawyers could say with confidence he was innocent. They could say he might not have received a fair trial. Later, however, credible evidence of innocence surfaced. An eyewitness told investigators she knew Burton and had seen the shooting but could not identify the shooter. The eyewitness had not been contacted before Burton's trial and therefore had not testified. Investigators also developed evidence pointing to someone else as the shooter, a man, now deceased, who had feuded with the victim and threatened to kill him.

So imagine the frustration of Burton's appellate lawyers—17 years into Burton's prison term—when three judges from the U.S. Court of Appeals for the Eighth Circuit said they also believed the defendant could be innocent but could do nothing about it.

Why not? Here are a few paragraphs excerpted from a longer opinion by the three judges:

"Debate has intensified in recent years as Congress and the federal courts have limited access to the writ in reaction to increasing numbers of habeas petitions. The limitations include a confounding array of procedural impediments that prevent consideration of the merits of claims, as well as substantive barriers that establish modes of review utterly inhospitable to prisoners. Many barriers and impediments represent sound efforts to curb the groundswell of frivolous and duplicative habeas petitions. But the writ of habeas corpus is not a one-way path designed to defeat prisoners' claims. Rather, our habeas jurisprudence is a balancing act requiring careful attention to each of the important, yet often opposing, principles at stake. Even as we screen meritless petitions, therefore, we must take care not to shut the door to prisoners whose claims cause us to doubt the fairness of their convictions.

"The present case suggests we may not yet have achieved the optimal balance. Darryl Burton's habeas petition depicts a troubling scenario. One cannot read the record in this case without developing a nagging suspicion that the wrong man may have been convicted of capital murder and armed criminal action in a Missouri courtroom. Burton was convicted on the strength of two eyewitness accounts. Since his trial and imprisonment, new evidence has come to light that shakes the limbs of the prosecution's case. One eyewitness has recanted and admitted perjury. The other eyewitness's veracity has been questioned by a compatriot who avers it was physically impossible for him to have seen the crime. A layperson would have little trouble concluding Burton should be permitted to present his evidence of innocence in *some* forum. Unfortunately, Burton's claims and evidence run headlong into the thicket of impediments erected by courts and by Congress. Burton's legal claims permit him no relief, even as the facts suggest he may well be innocent."

Burton's case is by no means unique. Jordan Anderson and Clyde Anderson, convicted of armed robbery in 1970 in Louisiana, were denied habeas corpus relief even though another federal appellate court conceded, as in Burton, that the state's evidence against the two was weak. For example, they were convicted on the basis of testimony from an 11-year-old girl who was only at the crime scene momentarily and saw the robber with a mask. A store employee later admitted he had identified the wrong men; what's more, a fellow inmate later confessed to the crime.

But the court felt that its hands were tied. "We do not gainsay petitioners' argument that the evidence upon which they were convicted was weak," the judges wrote. "Indeed, if we were reviewing this case on direct appeal to determine whether the evidence was sufficient to support their conviction, we cannot be certain that we would deny relief to these two defendants. We are not hearing a direct appeal, however, but are deciding the merits of a habeas corpus petition from a state prisoner. ... Therefore, on the basis of the relevant precedent in this circuit, we must affirm the district court's dismissal of the petition."

That was also another court's conclusion in the case of Richard Milone, who was convicted of murder in 1973 and denied habeas corpus relief in 1994 even though he had made a "credible claim" of actual innocence, supported by another man's confession to the murder, which he repeated several times before committing suicide in his jail cell in 1987. In rejecting Milone's appeal, the court expressed its sympathy for Milone's position but cited a Supreme Court ruling in *Herrera v. Collins* that "strongly suggests that actual innocence is not itself a ground for granting habeas relief in anything other than a capital case."

In Burton's case, the appellate judges expressed their uneasiness with the decision. "Burton's habeas petition troubles us because his legal claims do not provide an adequate foundation upon which to present his considerable claims of factual innocence. Though our jurisprudence offers Burton no relief, we express the hope that the state of Missouri may provide a forum (either judicial or executive) in which to consider the mounting evidence that Burton's conviction was procured by perjured or flawed eyewitness testimony." But no such forum has been provided. In April 2003, the U.S. Supreme Court turned away the last-chance appeal filed by Burton's defense attorney.

In cases such as these, where a mistake seems so evident, it seems reasonable to assume the prosecutor who filed the charge would find a way to minimize the injustice. That rarely happens, however. The finality of a jury verdict is a touchstone of the U.S. criminal justice system, and the procedures for changing the verdict are filled with obstacles and gaps. And in too many cases, that means the innocent must stay behind bars.

Shielding Misconduct
The law immunizes prosecutors from civil suits

A physician who botches an operation or an attorney in private practice whose incompetence costs his client a small fortune can both be sued for malpractice. A prosecutor who convicts a defendant of a crime he didn't commit, on the other hand, enjoys immunity from civil suits. That immunity was almost absolute, but a series of court rulings in the last decade have begun to whittle away at the protections for prosecutors who break rules in gaining convictions.

In 1976, the U.S. Supreme Court ruled in *Imbler v. Pachtman* that prosecutors should be protected by absolute immunity from civil lawsuits, reasoning that the threat of litigation from defendants might interfere with a prosecutor's job. The justices also assumed that supervisors and bar disciplinary boards would offer punishment enough to deter prosecutors from breaking rules. Research conducted since the *Imbler* decision suggests that in most prosecutors' offices and at most state disciplinary agencies, the justices' expectations are not being met: prosecutors are rarely disciplined for misconduct in the courtroom. The justices have not overridden the 1976 ruling.

In a separate opinion in the *Imbler* ruling, Justice Byron White concurred with the majority but wondered about the wisdom of extending absolute immunity to prosecutors who withheld evidence suggesting that a defendant was innocent. Prosecutors ought to live in fear that failure to disclose such evidence could lead to civil liability, White insisted. But twenty-seven years later, prosecutors have pretty much absolute immunity from civil lawsuits as long as they are acting as government advocates "intimately associated with the judicial phase of the criminal process."

After the *Imbler* ruling, various courts invoked absolute immunity for prosecutors who broke promises that they would not charge a suspect with a crime; presented false or misleading evidence to a grand jury; offered to drop charges if a defendant agreed to withdraw from a civil proceeding; shopped for an expert forensic witness until finding a sympathetic one, despite knowing that the expert used questionable methods; and, as Justice White had feared, withheld evidence suggesting innocence.

By 1991, however, enough splits had emerged within and between the circuit courts that the Supreme Court revisited immunity for prosecutors in a case called *Burns v. Reed*.

By and large, the Court upheld the principle, but with one exception: a prosecutor could be sued for his actions during the investigative, and not judicial, stage of a case.

Just two years later, in 1993, the U.S. Supreme Court ruled in another case involving the degree of immunity from civil liability protecting prosecutors. The dispute had its beginnings in an Illinois wrongful conviction case; the justices again found that immunity did not extend to actions prosecutors undertook while investigating a case.

In 1997, the Supreme Court heard the case of *Lynne Kalina v. Rodney Fletcher*, and found an instance in which a prosecutor could be held liable for her actions.

Fletcher was charged with stealing from a school and spent a day in jail after his arrest. A month later, Kalina, the prosecutor, dismissed the case. Fletcher sued Kalina, who asked that the lawsuit be dismissed. At issue were the documents Kalina filed to get an arrest warrant. Kalina contended that she had filed the documents as part of her official duties and enjoyed absolute immunity from liability. The trial court and an intermediate appellate court disagreed with Kalina. The U.S. Supreme Court accepted the case "because we have never squarely addressed the question whether a prosecutor may be held liable for conduct in obtaining an arrest warrant."

The justices said Kalina's "activities in connection with the preparation and filing of two of the three charging documents—the information and the motion for an arrest warrant—are protected by absolute immunity." A third document, however—a certification that the other documents were accurate—troubled the court. "Indeed, except for her act in personally attesting to the truth of the averments in the certification, it seems equally clear that the preparation and filing of the third document in the package was part of the advocate's function as well. The critical question, however, is whether she was acting as a complaining witness rather than a lawyer when she executed the certification under penalty of perjury."

Kalina offered the certification because it was local practice for somebody from the prosecutor's office to do so. That practice perhaps needed re-thinking, the justices said. When Kalina personally signed the certification, she was acting as a witness, not as an advocate. Therefore, she could not expect absolute immunity.

Much of the time when an aggrieved defendant sues a prosecutor, there is no monetary recovery or the outcome is shrouded in secrecy. Fletcher's lawsuit against Kalina, however, yielded payment to him in a public outcome. Norm Maleng, King County's elected prosecutor, apologized to Fletcher, as did Kalina separately. King County, Kalina's employer, paid Fletcher $162,500 to settle the lawsuit before trial.

A Short History of Exposing Misconduct
An unlikely cast of characters has shone a spotlight on bad prosecutors, and on occasion sparked reform

In January 1999, the *Chicago Tribune* published a five-part series of articles that found, in the paper's own words, "nearly 400 cases where prosecutors obtained homicide convictions by committing the most unforgivable kinds of deception. They hid evidence that could have set defendants free. They allowed witnesses to lie. All in defiance of the law. Prosecutors swear to seek the truth but instead many pursue convictions at any cost. The premium is on winning, not justice."

The series, reported and written by Maurice Possley and Ken Armstrong, documented 381 cases, going back to 1963, in which courts reversed murder convictions because prosecutors presented evidence they apparently knew to be false, or concealed evidence suggesting innocence, or both.

Then, in November 1999, the *Tribune* published another in-depth series by Armstrong and reporter Steve Mills that examined murder cases in which Illinois prosecutors, mostly in Cook County (Chicago), had charged a defendant with a capital crime and asked for the death penalty. The journalists identified 326 reversals attributed in whole or part to the conduct of the prosecutors.

As in the first series, the reporters named names—of prosecutors, incompetent or corrupt defense attorneys, police officers, forensic scientists, judges and others within the criminal justice system. They wrote about how prosecutors used confessions extracted through police torture, used perjured testimony of jailhouse informants seeking rewards, or used unreliable analyses from law enforcement forensic laboratories.

On January 19, 2000, Mills and Armstrong reported that former Chicago police officer Steve Manning had become the thirteenth Illinois Death Row inmate to be cleared, versus 12 executed. The *Tribune* had explained the holes in the case against Manning as part of the November series. On February 1, 2000, Mills and Armstrong reported probably the most consequential story that could arise from a journalistic expose: George Ryan, the Republican governor of Illinois who had previously supported the death penalty, announced a moratorium. He cited the work of the *Tribune* as the foundation of his decision.

In-depth, systematic scrutiny of prosecutors in specific districts like the *Tribune* investigation has been rare throughout the decades. But an unlikely cast of characters—including university professors, a judge, an author best known for creating a fictional defense attorney, and a handful of journalists—studied the issue of prosecutorial misconduct over the years, raising public awareness and on occasion sparking reforms.

The first in-depth examination was more than 70 years ago. In 1932, Yale University law professor Edwin M. Borchard wrote his book *Convicting the Innocent: Sixty-Five Actual Errors of Criminal Justice*. Borchard understood that many readers would find his case studies unbelievable, given the overwhelming faith the public had in the court system. As a prosecutor in Worcester County, Mass., put it, "Innocent men are never convicted. Don't worry about it, it never happens in the world. It is a physical impossibility."

It is unknown how that prosecutor reacted to Borchard's case studies, which included eight instances of defendants convicted of murder when the supposed victim turned up later, alive.

Borchard was charitable to prosecutors in passage after passage, noting how they were "obliged to take the evidence as presented...including the uncontrollable perjury of vengeful witnesses, and lay it before the jury without realization of its worthlessness. Except in the few cases where evidence is consciously suppressed or manufactured, bad faith is not necessarily attributable to the police or prosecution; it is the environment in which they live, with an undiscriminating public clamor for them to stamp out crime and make short shrift of suspects."

Borchard did point out, however, the self-interest that was also part of the environment: "It is common knowledge that the prosecuting technique in the United States is to regard a conviction as a personal victory calculated to enhance the prestige of the prosecutor."

Following in Borchard's wake was lawyer Erle Stanley Gardner, best known as the creator of the fictional defense attorney Perry Mason. Gardner used the proceeds of his novels to fund research into real life miscarriages of justice, and created the Court of Last Resort in the late 1940s, an unofficial tribunal that investigated suspected wrongful convictions.

In 1952, Gardner wrote a book about the tribunal; he also published numerous articles and paid for advertising campaigns that helped individual defendants receive justice. Gardner's efforts caught the public's imagination, but not even an author with Gardner's reach succeeded in reforming the systemic problems that led to unfair trials.

New York State Judge Jerome Frank collaborated with his daughter Barbara Frank, an attorney, to write the 1957 book *Not Guilty*. Like Borchard and Gardner, the Franks helped to set the standard for tracking misconduct. In addition to documenting cases in which individuals were denied a fair trial or wrongfully convicted, the Franks suggested reforms to the court system to prevent such miscarriages of justice in the future.

In the 1960s, others began considering the problem. Journalist Edward D. Radin carried on the public education campaign, turning up unfair trials and cases of actual innocence by tirelessly reading newspapers and magazines. Some publications, Radin found, "overlook or ignore such incidents in their own communities or states but print some of those that occur elsewhere. It is only by a daily culling of newspapers from many sections of the country that this finger pointing in other directions becomes obvious, and also it is only as the clippings mount that one realizes how often injustices do occur."

In 1964, Hugo Adam Bedau, a university philosophy professor, joined the public debate with his book *The Death Penalty in America.* Bedau approached prosecutorial conduct and actual innocence issues from an anti-death penalty perspective. The philosopher never lost interest in the subject. In 1987, he and sociology professor Michael L. Radelet collaborated on a *Stanford University Law Review* article about wrongful convictions that led to an impassioned rebuttal from U.S. Justice Department lawyers.

To reach a wider audience, Radelet and Bedau asked professional writer Constance E. Putnam, Bedau's wife, to help them with a book. *In Spite of Innocence: Erroneous Convictions in Capital Cases,* published in 1992, covered about 400 defendants, and expanded on the *Stanford University Law Review* article. Both Bedau, who retired from Tufts University, and Radelet, who consults with other researchers from the University of Colorado campus, continue to write and publish.

In Cook County, Ill., Rob Warden started reaching a small but intensely interested audience with his magazine *Chicago Lawyer,* founded in 1978. Year after year, he and his small staff exposed misconduct by police and prosecutors leading to unfair trials and sometimes wrongful convictions.

Warden began to achieve recognition outside Illinois after collaborating with David Protess, a freelance journalist and Northwestern University journalism professor. Protess, some of his students and Warden helped free innocents from prison while, amazingly, identifying the actual murderous perpetrators. During the 1990s, Protess and Warden collaborated on two best-selling books together, each book about a case of actual innocence.

After selling his magazine in 1989, Warden started changing the system from the inside, first as executive officer for the Cook County state's attorney, later as executive director of the Northwestern University Center on Wrongful Convictions, a position he still holds.

In 1991, Martin Yant, a Columbus, Ohio, journalist, published his book *Presumed Guilty: When Innocent People Are Wrongly Convicted* a compilation that resonated far beyond the borders of his state.

A Poisoned Prosecution
Misconduct in sexual abuse cases damages reputations—
and can ruin lives

In May 1999, Robert Wasser's life was turned upside down when Walworth County, Wis., Assistant District Attorney Diane Resch charged him with fourth-degree sexual assault. The charge stemmed from a complaint filed by Wasser's then 20-year-old adopted daughter Samantha (not her real name).

Wasser and his wife Bonnie had dedicated their adult lives to helping abused and neglected children. Over the years, the couple had adopted 22 children and were on the state's list of parents who take in special needs kids. The state would sometimes use them for emergency placement when children had nowhere else to go. When the Wassers adopted 14-year-old Samantha, they knew the risks. Her previous foster father had sexually assaulted her, and she would need special care. But they had had success raising similar adopted children and were confident they could help her.

Wasser's troubles began one weekend when Samantha was home from Wisconsin Lutheran College, a four-year, coed liberal arts school in Milwaukee. Wasser found a handwritten note from Samantha to her boyfriend, a man she would later marry, about dropping out of college and leaving Wisconsin together. Wasser confronted Samantha about the note. Later, he drove her back to college.

The drive to Milwaukee was tense—but still, the conflict with Samantha seemed minor to Wasser, considering her painful past. All that changed, however, a few months later, when an overzealous prosecutor with a history of misconduct and a series of mistruths and outright lies turned a minor dispute into a major crisis. While the charges against Wasser were eventually dismissed, he lost his job, his reputation was damaged, and he incurred the expense of a court battle. The woman who prosecuted him, and misled the court in the process, still has her job.

Aggressive advocacy—and misconduct

At a time when the nation was still trying to make sense of a series of highly charged and much publicized sexual abuse trials involving children—some of which would show how the original accusations were either coaxed by aggressive investigators or induced by questionable therapeutic techniques—some prosecutors continued to push for convictions with very questionable evidence. Resch, for one, remained a passionate prosecutor of alleged sexual abuse and had assumed responsibility for most of Walworth's sexual assault cases since joining the DA's office in 1992. Since then, the Wisconsin Court of Appeals has addressed her conduct at least seven times. In four of those appeals, judges ruled that her behavior warranted reversing the defendant's conviction. Two of the reversals involved alleged child sexual abuse.

Resch declined requests to comment for this report.

In 1994, appellate judges reversed a conviction Resch won against Andrew Torstenson for the sexual assault of a child. There had been no physical proof or eyewitness testimony; Resch's case rested mostly on the victim's statements. During the trial, Resch told the jury that the trial judge thought the victim's statements were "reliable," "credible" and "trustworthy." Defense counsel offered no objection and the trial judge did not admonish Resch, though he did tell the jury that the prosecutor's opinions and arguments were not evidence. Writing for a unanimous appeals court, Judge Richard S. Brown held, "When the prosecutor commented that the court had given a judicial imprimatur to [the victim's] credibility, the jury was effectively being told that [the victim] was truthful and, therefore, that the State's case was the truth." Resch's bolstering of the victim's statements denied Torstenson a fair trial, the court concluded. "In a credibility battle, we can hardly think this to be unprejudicial," Brown wrote.

In a 1998 burglary case, Resch withheld exculpatory police interviews from the defense. In reversing the conviction, the appeals court held that the interviews showed there was no "criminal intent" and "seriously" impeached a police officer, who was also a witness for the state.

In a 1997 case involving child and animal neglect, Resch used juvenile-court records she had obtained on the eve of the trial without notifying the defense counsel. Appellate Judge Harry G. Snyder wrote that the court had "no confidence in the outcome of the verdict" and reversed the conviction.

The year after Wisconsin State Legislature passed a law that allowed children as young as 10 to be convicted of serious sex crimes, Resch charged a 10-year-old boy with first-degree sexual assault.

The charges, which led to a three-day, non-jury trial in front of Walworth County Judge Robert Kennedy, stemmed from two separate incidents, both of which occurred while David played in his backyard with other children. In the first incident, he touched a next-door neighbor during a game of truth or dare. In the second, he created a new rule for a game of capture-the-flag—the girls had to lift their shirts when they were captured.

One of the girls said David touched her underneath the shirt.

Resch argued that the law does not distinguish between childhood sexual exploration and an adult with intent to be sexually aroused. "This is just as wrong as an adult playing these games with little kids," she told the court.

Kennedy ordered the boy to be placed on one-year supervision at home with psychological counseling, restitution and community service. The judge also ordered him to register as a sexual offender and provide a DNA sample.

The boy provided a DNA sample but appealed the order requiring him to register as a sex offender. In 2001, the Wisconsin Court of Appeals ruled in his favor.

"Resch just went for the throat and was treating him like he was 18," the boy's mother told the Center for Public Integrity. "She wasn't interested in the truth; no one was interested in the truth."

Sexual assault alleged

About a week after Wasser had spoken to Samantha about her intention to quit school, Samantha called to tell him she had dropped out of college and was living with her boyfriend. A month later, Bonnie Wasser received the first of many letters alleging sexual contact between Robert and Samantha.

"Ask christen Bob about his sinful relationship with his foster daughter, Sam," one of the typed letters said.

"You must condemned this man from the innocent children under his authority," said another.

Wasser's workplace and one of his three birth sons also received letters. Soon, the reason for the letters became apparent.

"We got a call in December from the guy she is with saying the harassment would go away for $500 a month," Wasser said. He also received a letter from Samantha asking for money to help pay bills.

One of the letters was dated January 9, 1999. That same day, Officer Jeff Recknagel interviewed Samantha and her boyfriend at the Fontana Police Department. The police had been contacted by a therapist Samantha was seeing. During the interview, Samantha claimed that Wasser had sexually assaulted her once when she was 19 years old and once again when she was 20.

When Recknagel interviewed Wasser at his home, Wasser told him the allegations were not only false but also indistinguishable from Samantha's allegations against her previous foster father.

"He didn't believe me," said Wasser.

In February 1999, Assistant District Attorney Diane Resch took the case.

In March, Wasser received a certified letter stating that Samantha was filing a civil suit against him for monetary compensation.

Two months later, Resch pressed criminal charges.

Wasser hired defense attorney David Danz, who had previously served as District Attorney, to represent him. Danz entered a not-guilty plea.

"Our lawyer told us the system worked," Bonnie Wasser said. "But I think I over-estimated the honesty of the system."

A culture of misconduct

Resch wasn't the only one at the Walworth County District Attorney's office with a recent history of aggressive prosecutions, error and misconduct. Since 1990—the year District Attorney Phillip Koss was elected to office—there have been at least 26 appellate decisions addressing alleged prosecutorial error. In the 20 years before that, there were three. In 11 of those 26 cases, judges ruled that the prosecutor's conduct required reversing the defendant's conviction.

The appellate court has addressed Koss's conduct in at least 11 cases. In five, the court ruled that his misconduct warranted reversing the defendant's conviction. Two reversals involved alleged child sexual assault.

In January 2003, for example, the Wisconsin appellate court reversed a conviction for sexual assault of a child because Koss convinced trial judge James Carlson to ignore a precedent-setting appellate decision, *Richard A.P.* That decision held that defendants in sexual assault cases must be allowed to use psychological experts in their defense. Koss apparently thought the decision was wrong.

"We are troubled by the district attorney's arguments that a trial court is free to ignore a published decision of the court of appeals," wrote Judge Snyder. "While the District Attorney may think that *Richard A.P.* was an 'obviously' wrong decision and contrary to nationwide precedent, it is the law."

In 1999, Koss prosecuted Mark Daer for sexually assaulting his eight-year-old step-daughter. The appellate court reversed Daer's conviction in August 2002 because Koss "prevented the real question of Daer's guilt from being fully tried." Among the incidents the court found problematic were "the prosecutor's improper focus during closing argument on [alleged perjury by Daer's wife] Trina Daer and the prosecutor's comment during closing argument that defense attorneys routinely trumpet their clients' innocence no matter what the evidence at trial."

In another case, which Koss prosecuted before his election to District Attorney, the appellate court reversed the defendant's conviction because Koss withheld evidence suggesting that the defendant was innocent.

"This type of abuse wasn't present before," said Defense Attorney Jeffrey Krebs, who has practiced in Walworth for about 18 years and is now the deputy assistant state public defender. "It has been going on since 1990—it starts at the top."

Koss said some defense attorneys might mistake his vigorous public advocacy for abuse.

"I believe we are aggressive on prosecuting child sexual assault cases," Koss said. "We've prosecuted cases that other counties would not."

Karen Barbour, a victim's advocate who has worked in Walworth for 26 years, agrees.

"They take these cases extremely seriously and they are very proactive as far as prosecution," she said. "They will take on many cases that other district attorney's would not consider prosecuting." She has worked closely with Koss in many cases involving children.

"I think he is very professional and takes his work very seriously," she said.

No Plea

In June, Resch offered Wasser a deal. He could plead guilty to one count and the state would not recommend a sentence, leaving that to the discretion of the judge. Wasser turned down the deal. For the next seven months, his case lingered in the system on various hearings and continuances.

On February 8, 2001, Resch offered Wasser a second deal. He could plead guilty to disorderly conduct, and the state would recommend a sentence of costs only. Again, Wasser turned her down: Wasser said he was not willing to plead guilty to something he did not do.

Five months later, Samantha dropped her civil suit, and Resch withdrew the offer.

"With the issue of money no longer looming over the case, the defense was without any motive for the victim to falsely accuse the defendant," Resch wrote in a report.

On October 11, with the trial date approaching, Danz confronted Resch with the crux of Wasser's defense—the similarity between Samantha's description of the sexual assault by her previous foster father James Schlosser and her allegations against Wasser. Both cases involved manual masturbation and ejaculation.

Diane Resch insisted that first Samantha then Diane Behrens, one of Samantha's previous foster mothers, said Schlosser had had sexual intercourse with her. Resch told Danz and Watson (and the court) that the Schlosser incidents "clearly involved sexual intercourse." Resch insisted the two assaults were entirely different. She told Danz she had spoken with Samantha, who had specifically told her the two assaults were different.

Danz sent Resch a fax transcript of their conversation together. He asked Resch to "call immediately" if she discovered that the two assaults were, in fact, similar. An hour later, Resch called Danz and said Samantha was in her office and had confirmed that the two assaults were "clearly" different.

The next day, armed with a transcript of the first foster father's trial that proved the allegations were similar, Danz went to Judge Michael Gibbs. At this point, Resch changed her story. She told the court that Samantha had never told her the assaults were different. She said it was actually Diane Behrens, one of Samantha's previous foster mothers, who had explained how the two assaults were different. She denied ever having told Danz otherwise.

Gibbs called an evidentiary hearing to determine the truth, and enjoined both sides from speaking to Diane Behrens or Samantha.

Because Danz would be a witness at the evidentiary hearing, Wasser hired local defense attorney Steven Watson to aid in his defense. Resch would also be a witness, so District Attorney Koss stepped in to aid in the prosecution.

Samantha and Behrens took the stand and denied telling Resch that the assaults were different. Behrens denied discussing the previous assault at all.

When District Attorney Koss asked Samantha to describe Wasser's assault, she instead described details of the allegations that led to her previous foster father's conviction. Samantha also testified that Resch never asked her about the differences in the two allegations.

Gibbs ended the evidentiary proceeding by asking all the attorneys not to talk to the witnesses while he decided on his ruling. "I don't want to see affidavits coming in with different versions," he said.

While waiting for Gibbs' ruling, Danz and Watson discovered a smoking gun. Officer Recknagel had interviewed Diane Behrens on June 30, 1999. He asked her about the similarities between Samantha's first father's conviction and her allegations against Wasser.

"Now is this the same type of sexual contact that her prior foster father had with her also?" asked Recknagel. "Yes it was," answered Behrens.

Resch had Recknagel's report of the interview all along.

In April, Gibbs issued an opinion dismissing with prejudice all charges against Wasser because of prosecutorial misconduct. (Courts rarely dismiss a case "with prejudice"; it means that a defendant cannot be retried. In Wasser's case, the judge cited the prosecutor's misconduct as the reason). Gibbs ruled that Resch provided false information and lied under oath in an effort to "cover up her misrepresentation to defense."

"The Court believes ADA Resch was dishonest with the Court and defense counsel," Gibbs wrote in his decision. "The Court finds that ADA Resch provided false information to the Court on October 12 and lied under oath on October 16.

"The misconduct has infected the proceedings with unfairness and has poisoned the entire atmosphere of the proceedings."

Permanent stain

Even with his charges dismissed, the court of public opinion continues to haunt Wasser. Before Resch filed the charges against him, he was the head director of a Milwaukee boarding school. Now he can't step foot on campus.

"It's a loss of profession," Wasser said. "I'm 59 years of age, and not too many people want to pick up a has-been." Wasser believes that the efforts he and his wife have made on behalf of children like Samantha made him particularly vulnerable to the charges that cost him his job. "[B]ecause we adopt children who have been abused, we're high risk for allegations."

Wasser filed a claim for damages against Walworth County, including Resch and Recknagel, for $910,000. In his claim, he stated that because of Resch's actions, he suffered significant injuries and damages, including humiliation and loss of future employment.

Koss suspended Resch with pay while he looked into her conduct in Wasser's case. The Office of Lawyer Regulations began its investigation by convening a small panel of clerks and attorneys from other counties to determine whether disciplinary action was warranted. A special prosecutor also investigated Resch's conduct to determine if criminal charges were appropriate.

During the OLR investigation, Judge Robert Kennedy, who served as Walworth County District Attorney from 1979 to 1985, wrote a letter to the OLR supporting Resch. A local newspaper had published Resch's endorsement of his judicial re-election campaign. So close is the relationship between Kennedy and Resch that local defense attorneys routinely charge judicial bias and request a different judge whenever the two are assigned to the same case.

"I am aware of an ethics rule that indicated that judges should not volunteer to testify as character witnesses," Kennedy's letter says. "If it does apply, then I must ask you to disregard this letter and return it to me." He closes the letter by "stressing the fact that her character for truthfulness and honesty both in and outside the courtroom to my knowledge is above reproach."

Although several sources with knowledge of the situation told the Center that the panel unanimously agreed to disbar her, Resch has received no disciplinary action.

None of the sources could explain why Resch received no punishment. The special prosecutor did not press criminal charges, and Koss later determined that Resch's behavior did not warrant discipline.

After receiving notice that Resch would receive no disciplinary action, Steve Watson closed his law practice and moved to Vermont. "I just couldn't stomach it anymore," Watson said. Even with half a country between him and Walworth, he said the injustice he witnessed still upsets him. As recently as February of this year, he wrote a letter to the OLR appealing their decision. The OLR declined to revisit the matter.

"A circuit judge had made a specific finding of fact that [Resch] had lied, OLR's own investigative panel reached the same conclusion, and yet the final decision reached the opposite conclusion and gave no explanation whatsoever," Watson wrote.

The next day, OLR informed Watson that they would not re-open the case. The director of OLR "did not believe that this office could prove by clear, satisfactory, and convincing evidence that Ms. Resch had made a misrepresentation."

Resch is currently prosecuting felonies, including sexual assaults of children, in Walworth County. As recently as February, she retried a defendant whose conviction had been reversed due to her conduct.

Changing an Office's Culture
In San Diego County, prosecutors have tried to do the right thing—but haven't always succeeded

S ince 1970, appellate judges ruled on allegations of prosecutorial error or misconduct allegations in 45 San Diego County cases, of which eight led to reversals, dismissals or acquittals. As in other jurisdictions studied by the Center for Public
Integrity, the totals come solely from appellate opinions. San Diego County defense
lawyers provided numerous examples of error or misconduct at the pre-trial or trial stage.

But San Diego stands out amidst the 2,341 jurisdictions the Center researched for
its attempts over the last 30 years to do things differently—in part because the office of
district attorney has been held by prosecutors who have attempted to make the office
more accountable. Perhaps a reflection of their success lies in this fact: the citizenry of
San Diego County became so educated about prosecutorial misconduct that when it did
occur, they were ready to hold the district attorney responsible and vote him out of
office, no matter his accomplishments or intentions.

The changes began with the election in 1970 of Edwin L. Miller Jr., who would go
on to serve for 24 years. During his tenure, Miller made drastic changes to the office, in
part by stressing specialization and career ladders. He encouraged young trial prosecutors who showed talent to stay on permanently, thus solidifying the culture at the top. He
introduced some reforms—notably the compilation of an office manual for prosecutors,
and the publication of a journal, *Law Enforcement Quarterly*, first published by the San
Diego District Attorney's office in 1971. (Originally a specialized journal for legal professionals, in 1989 it became a more approachable magazine for general readers.)

Miller built a national reputation as an honest, reform-minded public official. True,
there were instances of misconduct among the career prosecutors who worked for him.
In a 1976 murder trial, L. Forrest Price, then an 11-year veteran prosecutor hired by
Miller's predecessor, withheld a document from the defense that contradicted a witness'
testimony. Unbeknownst to Price, defense counsel got a copy of the document from the
witness himself; later, Price supplied a doctored version. Jurors, unaware of the failure
to disclose or the alteration, found the defendant guilty. Before sentencing, Price quiet-

ly offered a deal directly to the defendant—if he would refrain from appealing, perhaps a favorable sentence would result. Defense counsel knew nothing about the offer. In any event, the deal fell through.

Ultimately, Price's behavior was exposed and the California attorney general charged him with a felony. After a jury acquitted him, Price sought reinstatement to his position. The civil service commission ruled in Price's favor. But Miller was opposed and refused to reinstate him.

Such instances did little to tarnish Miller's reputation. In four of his reelection campaigns, he ran unopposed, and he won plaudits from his fellow prosecutors nationwide.

All that changed with the case of Dale Akiki.

Near what turned out to be the end of Miller's tenure, the prosecution of the developmentally disabled Akiki for allegedly molesting youngsters at a church day care center fell apart in the courtroom. There was no physical evidence in the case, which rested largely on testimony from children. Lawyers inside and outside the office warned Miller that he was making a mistake by taking the case to trial. But Miller and several deputies pushed ahead. Despite weeks of testimony from children about Akiki's depredations, the jury acquitted him in less than a day. Later, Akiki won a large financial settlement from San Diego County for wrongful prosecution.

Miller acknowledged responsibility for the case, and promised changes in the way the office handled allegations of child molestation. In the 1994 election, his opponents made an issue of the case. In a primary field of five candidates, Miller placed fourth, ending his tenure as San Diego's district attorney. Paul J. Pfingst, a trial prosecutor hired by Miller who had since entered private practice, mounted an electoral challenge to his former boss, and won.

Miller felt dismay and anger that decades of what he considered exemplary service seemed forgotten because of one case that, while admittedly problematic given the difficulties connected with pre-school witnesses, appeared solid to him and his trial prosecutor. He disputed the notion that prosecutorial misconduct was something to worry about in San Diego County. The only instance of unambiguous misconduct he encountered, he said, involved L. Forrest Price, and he had moved quickly to fire Price.

Still, other instances of misconduct under Miller's reign would surface after his departure and plague his successor. The most significant were against James M. V. Fitzpatrick, a prosecutor in the office's gang unit and a hire of Miller's. In 1997, for example, a California appeals court vacated a murder conviction Fitzpatrick had obtained against Jemal M. Kasim in connection with a 1989 shooting. During an evidentiary hearing, it emerged that Fitzpatrick had allegedly intervened with the Immigration and Naturalization Service on behalf of one of his witnesses. The court learned about the intervention not because of any disclosure by Fitzpatrick, but because an INS lawyer came forward.

While the Kasim case played out, another of Fitzpatrick's convictions was reversed when a trial judge found that the prosecutor had misled defense counsel. Soon after the two cases, the San Diego County Civil Service Commission recommended that Fitzpatrick be fired, and Pfingst, who by that time had taken over for Miller as district attorney, cut him loose.

Pfingst continued to improve the image of the prosecutor's office. In the late 1990s, he and his staff initiated post-conviction DNA reviews of 766 pre-1992 cases. Before that year, DNA testing was normally unavailable or, if available, too primitive to be relied upon. George (Woody) Clarke and Lisa Weinreb, deputy district attorneys, took charge of the effort, which has since been emulated by prosecutors' offices across the nation. The results have not been dramatic. Case reviews have led to the realization that either no testable DNA exists or that testing will fail to produce a certain answer of innocence or guilt. Still, the effort is playing a role, however small thus far, in guarding against the San Diego County district attorney being complicit in the long-term incarceration of an innocent defendant.

Pfingst improved upon Miller's office manual. The thick loose leaf notebook, called the Legal Policies Guide, was researched and written by about two dozen lawyers in the office. It opens with a chapter on "crime charging," which discusses when to issue a case as a felony, when as a misdemeanor, for 20 different types of crimes. The second chapter focuses on two types of crimes, homicides and sexual assaults. The remaining chapters examine the operations of special teams within the office; disposing of felonies and misdemeanors; using subpoenas wisely; what must be disclosed to the defense in a process called "discovery"; victim and witness issues; pre-trial preliminary hearing procedures; grand juries; trial conduct; writs; appeals; and a collection of directives on specific additional matters going back to 1995.

Pfingst also allowed television producers to follow trial prosecutors on their rounds, gathering footage for the NBC-TV show "Crime and Punishment." The show aired for 13 Sunday nights during summer 2002. Without question, the show contributed to educating the general citizenry about the criminal justice system. And Pfingst made Miller's *Law Enforcement Quarterly* publication available on the Internet.

Amidst the reforms and improvements, the appearance of prosecutorial error and misconduct seemed surprising with Pfingst at the helm, just as it had during Miller's tenure. But, just as one instance would start fading from memory, another would arise. Additional questionable conduct by gang unit prosecutors that occurred during Miller's tenure surfaced publicly after Pfingst succeeded him—once again casting a shadow on the two men's considerable accomplishments.

Much of the controversy swirled around prosecutor Keith Burt, Fitzpatrick's supervisor, during proceedings against multiple defendants charged with murdering a police officer during 1988. A 1991 trial of one defendant ended with a deadlocked jury. Later the same year, the prosecution persuaded a grand jury to re-indict that defendant, along with five other men. Burt relied heavily on the testimony of a gang member turned informant. The jury eventually convicted three defendants of conspiracy and murder, one defendant of conspiracy only. The jury failed to reach unanimity on a fifth defendant's fate, and acquitted the sixth.

As the appeals progressed, the trial judge, troubled by what he had seen and heard, asked the state attorney general to investigate the prosecutor. Reports emerged that Burt allowed his informant, imprisoned for a crime other than the murder of the police officer, to engage in sexual intercourse while visiting the prosecutor's office. The trial judge opened an evidentiary hearing during 1998; he heard from 52 witnesses and examined hundreds of exhibits. The judge eventually recommended the convictions be reversed because of the prosecutor's conduct.

An appellate court weighed in by officially overturning the convictions. If any retrials were to occur, they would be handled by the attorney general, not Pfingst's prosecutors. Eventually, the attorney general decided against re-trials. In an extraordinary admission, the attorney general told the court, "The fact is, not one of these defendants has ever been proven to be the person who shot Officer Hartless. The district attorney could not establish this fact in two trials, and the attorney general cannot do so now." Pfingst's office issued a statement: "I'm not sure we would make the same decision, but it's [the attorney general's] decision, one honestly reached, and it deserves to be respected."

Unlike Fitzpatrick, Burt kept his prosecutor's position, though he eventually accepted a demotion within the office.

Another blow to Pfingst came in 2002 when, as he sought re-election, an appellate court made a finding of misconduct by one of his prosecutors. The ruling was not the only sign of trouble for Pfingst—about two-thirds of his deputies publicly opposed his re-election, citing his management style. Pfingst blamed the inability of the prosecutors to win pay raises from the county for their opposition, and said such matters had little to do with him. The complaints of those he supervised combined with the misconduct ruling dimmed his chances for winning another term.

The ruling involved John Lewis Tolliver's robbery-assault trial. Tolliver appealed, alleging misconduct by trial prosecutor Sophia Roach, who had been hired during Pfingst's tenure, as well as ineffectiveness by his defense counsel for failure to object to the purported misconduct.

Roach had said to the alibi witness, "You're pretty uncomfortable up there right now, aren't you?" The witness replied, "I'm fine," at which point Roach countered, "Does it make you nervous when you lie in front of the jury? Does it? No? It's easy to lie to the jury?" At one point during the trial, the judge called Roach to the bench, telling her, "You're so close to a mistrial. Do you have any idea?" Roach apologized to the judge, who in turn told the jury to disregard the prosecutor's previous question because it was "totally improper." The judge intervened at other junctures, especially because Tolliver's defense lawyer was not objecting.

The appellate judges overturned Tolliver's conviction, commenting "The prosecutor called Tolliver's alibi witness ... a liar while the witness was on the stand, and suggested to the jury that the witness was comfortable lying to them."

In an interview with the Center, Roach said the Tolliver case was the first felony reversal she had experienced during five years as a trial prosecutor. "It's so hard to think of anybody thinking of me as unethical," Roach said. Her immediate reaction to the appellate opinion was "shock," followed by "disappointment." She said she expects the ruling to "have a devastating and lasting effect."

As a result of the reversal, Roach and her colleagues in the San Diego County office received new instruction on what kinds of questions they can ask during cross-examination.

Pfingst also received bad publicity for a prosecution in a high profile case that collapsed before it reached the courtroom. San Diego County prosecutors charged a 14-year-old boy with the murder of his 12-year-old sister in their home, despite the lack of physical evidence, as well the existence of evidence that pointed to a different suspect. Defense counsel for the boy eventually forced DNA testing which placed the other suspect—a drifter with no connection to the family—in proximity to the victim. The case against the victim's brother evaporated before trial. Given its poor performance, Pfingst's office lost jurisdiction of the case to the state attorney general's prosecutors.

The conduct of the San Diego County district attorney's office in the case became material for lots of unflattering media headlines, which overshadowed Pfingst's accomplishments. At the beginning of 2003, Pfingst handed over his district attorney title to challenger Bonnie Dumanis.

Inside an Office
An Elected Prosecutor Explains

Jennifer M. Joyce, the current elected circuit attorney in St. Louis, oversees an office whose prosecutors, the Center for Public Integrity found, were challenged at least 167 times for alleged prosecutorial misconduct before she took office. Defendants were acquitted or had their convictions reversed in 29 of those cases. About halfway through her four-year term, Joyce and her staff seem acutely aware of the challenge ahead as they try to improve the situation in their home city.

The task is a daunting one. The top person in the office has a difficult job that tends to become more difficult every decade. That is especially so in major metropolitan areas, where the top prosecutor must manage hundreds of lawyers and support staff with a budget that always seems inadequate, deal with horrific crimes almost every day, think about prevention as well as conviction, all the while balancing the obligation to serve justice with the unavoidable scrutiny of won-lost statistics that become a factor in re-election campaigns. The difficulty has grown in medium-sized and small jurisdictions as well.

Frank Conley, just retired as chief judge of Boone County, Mo., after three decades on the bench, recalled his two terms as the elected prosecuting attorney after his 1962 victory. "In a full eight years as prosecutor, I had two legitimate armed robberies," Conley said. "Now, we have an armed robbery every night. We were just a little town back then." Today, Columbia, the seat of Boone County and its dominant incorporated area, has a population of about 80,000. "Substance abuse and the transient nature of our communities today, where you're here today and gone tomorrow, all of that has contributed to a lot of the problems we've seen," Conley said. "There is no sense of community in the sense that we knew it 30 or 40 or 50 years ago. It is gloomy."

Joyce, whose office is accountable to 333,960 citizens of St. Louis, is well aware of those problems.

Arrests by the police come first to Joyce's warrant office, which she calls "the sociological emergency room of St. Louis." Prosecutors normally have only a day to apply for a warrant after the police make an arrest. The warrant officer typically hears from the arresting officer, eyewitnesses if any, and the victim—if the victim is alive and able to talk. Joyce's staff initiates about 4,000 misdemeanor cases and about 5,000 felony cases annually.

Then the question becomes how to handle each case. Internally, a review committee of senior prosecutors meets weekly to determine whether the evidence is legally sufficient, and to do their best to see that similar cases receive similar treatment. The review committee members work from a sheet that includes a recommendation from the prosecutor most likely to handle the trial if the case goes that far, and an independent recommendation from another prosecutor known as the "evaluator." In addition to those two opinions, the sheet reveals factual information when relevant, such as other pending cases against the accused, prior convictions, co-defendants, whether the defendant made a statement, whether anybody identified the defendant and in what manner (line-up, show-up, photo spread, acquaintance), the nature of the forensic evidence, evidentiary and other issues of law, as well as who will probably serve as defense attorney. The review committee concentrates on felonies in which the prosecutor is probably going to seek prison time, rather than probation. Many of those cases end with plea agreements. About 250 felonies each year go to trial.

Like every elected prosecutor, one of Joyce's largest responsibilities—and perhaps her greatest chance of making an impact on her office—is deciding whom to hire. Joyce explained in an interview with the Center that about half of the new lawyers joining her staff are right out of law school, while the other half have made lateral moves. There is not an official office training manual—as there is in many California jurisdictions, for example—but the new prosecutors attend weekly training sessions at the office, travel to a national advocacy institute in Columbia, S.C., sit as second chair in at least two misdemeanor or felony trials and, in many instances, are sent to specialized units for training in handling certain kinds of cases, such as sex crimes.

A high turnover rate complicates any elected prosecutor's task. Joyce recognizes that turnover might be high because of relatively meager salaries compared to the private sector, as well as hires who want a lot of trial experience quickly to make them more attractive to future employers. Some of the new hires, however, will become career prosecutors; for them, Joyce said, "It's a calling."

Turning on Their Own

A group of former prosecutors cites a colleague's pattern of misconduct

While it is not unusual for an amicus curiae brief to be filed in a U.S. Supreme Court case, one such brief, filed on behalf of a Tennessee death row inmate, is unique both for its content and for the men who filed it. Six former Tennessee prosecutors argued, not on behalf of their state or the prosecutor, John Zimmermann, who won the conviction and death sentence against Abu-Ali Abdur'Rahman, but for the defendant. The six made the pattern of behavior of Zimmermann, a prosecutor in Davidson County (Nashville), Tenn., the central issue of their brief.

The U.S. Supreme Court listened to oral arguments in the Abdur'Rahman case in November 2002. Before reaching the highest court, the murder case wound its way through Tennessee's courts during the 1980s, 1990s and into the new century. The defendant in what is arguably Zimmermann's highest-profile case ever was born James Lee Jones. He found himself on death row after being convicted by a jury of murdering a man and wounding his female companion during an armed robbery. The Tennessee Supreme Court upheld the conviction in 1990, despite finding that Zimmermann's conduct in the case had crossed the line. In 1998, a U.S. District Court judge questioned Zimmermann's conduct in the same case, but did not give the defendant his desired result.

As knowledge of Zimmermann's behavior in the Abdur'Rahman case spread—knowledge supplemented by accounts of his behavior in other unrelated cases—the appeal to the U.S. Supreme Court started taking shape. The six former prosecutors, who constitute a who's who of the Tennessee legal profession, wrote in their brief, "All of us handled serious felonies and several of us handled capital matters when we served as prosecutors. ... While the consequence of prosecutorial misconduct is serious in any criminal prosecution, it is harrowing in a capital case. ... The prosecution ... fell far short of the standards of our state court system and, indeed, below what we understand the federal constitutional minimum standards to be. In our view, the record below taints all members of the Tennessee Bar."

The former prosecutors' brief alleged misconduct by Zimmermann at nearly every step. "Early in his investigation," they wrote, "the prosecutor recognized flaws in his case for a death sentence ... The scientific evidence strongly suggested that [Abdur'Rahman] was not the stabber, raising doubts the prosecutor knew would preclude capital punishment. The evidence ... indicates that the prosecutor masked the weaknesses in his case by suppressing key documents and presenting misleading testimony from an accomplice."

Zimmermann's questionable actions continued after Abdur'Rahman was convicted, awaiting sentence. "The prosecutor relied heavily on a prior homicide conviction in his request for the death penalty. In order to prevent the defendant from explaining mitigating facts concerning this prior offense, the prosecutor misrepresented those facts to defense counsel and falsely represented that an FBI agent would testify to the prosecutor's version of the events if the defense put those circumstances at issue."

The previous killing involving the defendant occurred in 1972, inside a federal prison. Zimmermann obtained the transcript of the trial connected to that 1972 death, but did not disclose the transcript to defense counsel. From reading the transcript, Zimmermann should have known that the fatal fight resulted from rumors of homosexual conduct, which is not what Zimmermann reportedly told defense counsel—that the death resulted from "a turf war in the prison between the two gangs as to who would control the drug trade" there. Zimmermann reportedly made that statement with an FBI agent present, an agent listed by the prosecutor as a witness against Abdur'Rahman.

The six former prosecutors wrote that in their experience, "the existence of a prior homicide, particularly one in prison, is a significant factor in the jury's determination whether life imprisonment is sufficient to guarantee the safety of the community. A killing over gangs and drugs presents a very different picture of the cold-bloodedness and dangerousness of a defendant than does an outburst stemming from a series of homosexual assaults on the defendant while he was incarcerated and unable to escape from them." Zimmermann's characterization of Abdur'Rahman's previous crime might have persuaded the jurors to impose a death sentence, the brief states.

"The prosecutor's misconduct was egregious," the six former prosecutors wrote. "If, as it appears, he made a representation to defense counsel he knew to be false in order to cut off an avenue of defense, that falsehood violates all standards of professional conduct."

Furthermore, the brief continued, Zimmermann's alleged misrepresentation of the 1972 prison death "was part of an even bigger distortion. The prosecutor systematically suppressed and misrepresented the evidence of [defendant's] mental illness," including its relationship to his crimes. The former prosecutors wrote that Zimmermann knew from the 1972 trial transcript the defendant pled not guilty by reason of insanity. Still,

Zimmermann reportedly told authorities while prosecuting the later murder that Abdur'Rahman never relied on an insanity defense in 1972. The result of Zimmermann's misrepresentation, the brief says, is that mental health professionals evaluating the defendant's competency to stand trial reached faulty conclusions based on faulty information.

A large portion of the brief uses Zimmermann's own words and actions to question his credibility. For example, Zimmermann allegedly knew he could have difficulty proving the defendant wielded the murder weapon, a knife, because an accomplice with credibility problems provided an explanation for the blood spatter that seems to belie the forensic evidence. Zimmermann "shielded from the defense and the jury this major weakness in his case," the six former prosecutors say. "The jury heard none of the evidence establishing that the person who did the stabbing would have been covered with blood, that [Abdur'Rahman's] long black coat had no traces of blood, and that witnesses saw [him] in the long black coat and did not see him remove it."

The brief attributes ill intentions to Zimmermann at almost every turn. For example, prosecutors wrote that Zimmermann "withheld from trial counsel the lab report showing no blood on [Abdur'Rahman's] coat, pants and shoes; the prosecutor gave this report to [Abdur'Rahman's] original lawyer, but did not give it to ... trial counsel, who requested discovery." The U.S. District Court ruled that the lab report Zimmermann supplied to the original lawyer on the case sufficed—no discovery violation, no misconduct. The six former prosecutors retort in their brief, "The district court ruled that defense counsel was ineffective for failing to obtain the report. The district court did not rule on the prosecutor's purposeful distortion of the evidence concerning the identity of the stabber, of which the withholding of the lab report was only one aspect."

The brief turns the ineffective assistance of defense counsel against Zimmermann as well: "Even though the prosecutor withheld crucial police reports and other documents, competent defense counsel might have learned enough about the facts to challenge the prosecutor's version of events. The prosecutor realized that defense counsel knew little about the facts, and exploited that lack of preparation. The prosecutor's conduct was no less improper because competent counsel might have minimized the damage. In fact ... the prosecutor's exploitation of defense counsel's inadequacies in order to win at any cost was a gross deviation from his obligation to seek justice."

On December 10, 2002, the U.S. Supreme Court, without explanation by the majority, dismissed the writ of certiorari as improvidently granted, meaning they decided not to rule on the merits of Abdur'Rahman's appeal. Justice John Stevens dissented, writing that the majority "presumably" dismissed the writ because of technical jurisdictional issues.

The Abdur'Rahman case is not the only time Zimmermann might have bent rules in pursuit of a conviction. In 2001, the Tennessee Court of Criminal Appeals commented on Zimmermann's conduct in connection with the conviction of Frank Michael Vukelich for conspiracy to deliver marijuana and money laundering. After a hung jury in the initial trial, a second trial began. During the first trial, Zimmermann had elicited testimony from a witness that he and Vukelich smoked marijuana together. The defense objected, and the judge sustained the objection. In the second trial, Zimmermann asked a similar question of the same witness, who testified the same way. After a defense objection, the trial judge admonished Zimmermann. The prosecutor apologized, saying he had forgotten the trial court's earlier ruling.

In 1999, the Tennessee Supreme Court upheld the murder conviction of Donald Ray Middlebrooks, despite the court's agreement with the defendant that Zimmermann crossed the line during closing argument to the jury. Middlebrooks said Zimmermann made inflammatory references to Biblical passages and to the desire of the victim's family for a death sentence. The appellate judges ruled Zimmermann offered "an improper characterization" of the family's views, but decided the remark should be placed in the harmless error category. As for the Bible passages, the judges said, "We have condemned Biblical and scriptural references in a prosecutor's closing argument so frequently that it is difficult not to conclude that the remarks in this case were made either with blatant disregard for our decisions or a level of astonishing ignorance of the state of the law ... As we have reiterated time and time again, the prosecutor has a legal and ethical duty to refrain from this sort of misconduct." Despite the strongly worded admonition, the court said the remarks should not result in a reversal of the conviction.

About the Middlebrooks case, Zimmermann notes that his reference to Biblical passages came in rebuttal to defense counsel references to the same holy book. In retrospect, Zimmermann says, "There is no doubt now that my rejoinder in the heat of the trial to the improper remarks of the defense counsel were improper." Still, Zimmermann says, he believed at the time he had to rebut in some fashion, because it appeared defense counsel's Biblical references had made a positive impression on some of the jurors.

Zimmermann, who has said little publicly about the allegations in the prosecutors' brief, responded to the Center for Public Integrity's request for comment. He counters every point in the brief from the six former prosecutors, in both the Abdur'Rahman case and the other cases mentioned. An overarching point made by Zimmermann is that no court examining the Abdur'Rahman record has found reason to reverse the conviction or the death sentence as a result of the prosecutor's conduct.

Regarding the allegation he "withheld and misrepresented evidence to convince the trial jury that [Abdur'Rahman] rather than an accomplice [Miller] performed the stabbing," Zimmermann points out what he says are errors of fact as well as mistaken conclusions. For example, the brief to the U.S. Supreme Court says the clothing Miller wore during the crime "was never located or tested for blood." Zimmermann says that police seized the jacket from Miller's car, later introducing it as evidence at trial. Various lawyers for Abdur'Rahman have seen the jacket, he told the Center. He presumes they never took it away for testing because a visual inspection shows no sign of blood. Given that Abdur'Rahman's expert witness on blood spatter testified the actual murderer would be covered with the substance, Zimmermann thinks he knows why the defense never tested Miller's jacket: If Abdur'Rahman is innocent because his coat was clean, then Miller must be presumed innocent, too. But that argument might not play well to a jury, because the facts are undisputed that one of the two men is a murderer.

Zimmermann supplied detailed information to rebut the allegations that he failed to disclose a laboratory report showing no blood on Abdur'Rahman's clothing. Abdur'Rahman's first attorney received the report, and has testified he transmitted case files to his successor. Zimmermann provided a letter to the successor attorney after receiving a discovery request. The letter says the information requested is available from the court and the initial defense lawyer. Zimmermann then adds, "If you want us to photocopy those for you and submit them to you, we will be happy to do so."

Zimmermann provided similarly detailed responses to every allegation made against him concerning the Abdur'Rahman case. He also addressed the additional cases he prosecuted which constituted, for the six former prosecutors, his "history of misconduct" similar to what is alleged in the Abdur'Rahman case.

In 2001, the Tennessee Court of Criminal Appeals reversed the murder conviction of Claude Francis Garrett, a case mentioned in the prosecutors' brief as one in which Zimmermann appears to have knowingly misrepresented forensic evidence.

Zimmermann told the jury that Garrett locked the victim in a room, then set the house afire. Three documents figure in the debate over whether the prosecution violated disclosure rules. While addressing all three documents, the appellate judges focused on the 11-page report suggesting the door was unlocked.

"The evidence ... showed that the prosecutor led defense counsel to believe that the state had no information about the locked or unlocked status of the utility room door. However, at trial the State's witnesses testified that the utility room door was locked and the prosecutor submitted to the jury as the theory of the state's case that the defendant locked the victim in the utility room and set the house on fire. Therefore, the state did have, prior to trial, information that the door was locked. ... [The state] also possessed the ... report which indicated otherwise—that [the] fire captain ... who was the first to enter the utility room and find the victim's body, found the door unlocked." When questioned after trial about why he excluded the 11-page report from discovery to the defense, Zimmermann said he believed the detective's recollection of his discussion with the fire captain to be vague, while the fire captain insisted he said nothing about an unlocked door.

The appellate judges commented they felt "extremely troubled with ... Zimmermann's decision to himself determine the reliability of the evidence and to refuse to turn over evidence he believes is unreliable, especially when the evidence is requested and is exculpatory."

In 2002, the Tennessee Supreme Court Disciplinary Board of Professional Responsibility censured Zimmermann in connection with the Garrett case, sending notice to judges and journalists about the prosecutor's misconduct.

About his censure by the disciplinary board for his conduct in the Garrett case, Zimmermann explained that he did not share the pre-trial statement of a police detective who talked to a firefighter because the document was inadmissible. Zimmermann said the firefighter denied the accuracy of the detective's written account, and the detective testified at a post-conviction hearing that he could not be certain of the accuracy himself. So why did the disciplinary board publicly censure Zimmermann? He said the answer is simple—various parties viewed the facts differently. "The trial court ruled that the 'impeachment' evidence was not material because it would have been inadmissible ... and held there was no Brady violation by me. The state attorney general wrote in his brief on appeal that the non-disclosure did not violate Brady. The Court of Criminal Appeals disagreed, and I received a public censure from the disciplinary board."

Playing By the Rules
Even when a prosecutor tries to do everything right,
the wrong person may still be convicted

The American justice system is designed to err on the side of allowing the guilty to go free rather than incarcerate the innocent. But when an innocent defendant enters the criminal justice system, grievous mistakes can occur, even when prosecutors play by the rules. In some cases the prosecutor simply could not have foreseen the grievous mistake.

Gary Delsohn, a *Sacramento Bee* reporter, reached that conclusion after intensive research into the wrongful conviction of David Jonathan Quindt by trial prosecutor Mark Curry. Delsohn obtained special access to the Sacramento district attorney's office while researching a book, "The Prosecutors: A Year in the Life of a District Attorney's Office," scheduled for publication by Dutton in August 2003. Delsohn's access gave him unique insight into the Quindt case, as well as a close look at the inner workings of a prosecutor's office.

Delsohn published an account of the Quindt case during 2002 in the quarterly magazine of the Alicia Patterson Foundation, an organization that gives financial support to journalists working on major projects. In an interview with the Center for Public Integrity, Curry said he has no quarrel with Delsohn's findings.

The crime leading to Quindt's murder conviction occurred Oct. 6, 1998, at a middle-class home in suburban Sacramento. The family living there grew high-quality marijuana, which several people knew about. Three armed men burst into the house at about 2:30 a.m., demanding the marijuana from the first occupants they saw—a 15-year-old girl who lived there and an 18-year-old male friend of her older brother. That male friend, Riley Haeling, a high school graduate working with disabled children, ended up dead, his body riddled with five bullets.

Police had no solid leads. A police sketch based on the description provided by the 15-year-old girl looked something like Quindt. Police were not totally surprised, knowing Quindt as a 21-year-old local punk who had started a suburban gang and worked at an equipment rental company. When police questioned Quindt, he stated his innocence.

But Quindt started acting in what detectives considered a suspicious manner by calling repeatedly to ask what they knew and to suggest leads.

Several months later, Quindt's name surfaced again. The information came from a Quindt acquaintance who told police that before the murder, he gave Quindt two guns. The day after the killing, the informant said, Quindt asked a different acquaintance to dispose of the guns. Furthermore, the informant said, soon after the murder he had purchased marijuana from a Quindt friend, Anthony Salcedo, age 17, a high school student who also had access to the guns.

Four months after the murder, police arrested Quindt and Salcedo. Curry tried Quindt during November 1999. At trial, the 15-year-old girl identified Quindt as one of the shooters. On Dec. 2, after three days of deliberation, the jury voted guilty. The prosecutor planned to seek a life sentence for Quindt. Salcedo would be tried separately, soon. Curry went home to enjoy the Christmas season.

With Christmas over, Curry took a call in his office. The prosecutor heard the voice of a 20-year-old petty criminal who had fed useful information to Curry in the past. "I know who committed the murder," the caller told Curry. "It is a different group of people than you have in custody for the crime."

Curry had no reason to believe the informant, who seemed motivated by a $10,000 reward originally offered by the family of the murdered 18-year-old. Still, Curry took some extraordinary steps: he started checking into the informant's claims and he asked that Quindt's formal sentencing be postponed.

Bit by bit, the informant told Curry the identities of the alleged actual perpetrators, men whose names had never arisen during the original investigation.

Further detective work seemed to confirm the informant's account. The prosecutor's office asked that Quindt be released from prison, and charged four other men with the crime. Those charges led to convictions by juries. According to Delsohn and Curry himself, the prosecutor suffered no long-term repercussions from originally convicting the wrong man.

Appendix

Methodology
How the Center compiled data for these articles

District Attorney. State's Attorney. Commonwealth's Attorney. County Attorney. Local prosecutors' job titles may differ from state to state, but they all share one basic function: to act as the public's advocate in the resolution of criminal cases.

Prosecutors wield tremendous power. After a suspect is arrested, prosecutors act as de facto judge and jury, deciding whether to charge the suspect with a crime, whether to offer a pre-trial deal, and, if so, the terms of the deal. In most jurisdictions, at least 95 percent of the cases that pour in from the police every day never reach a jury. The only trial those defendants receive takes place in the prosecutor's office.

The National District Attorneys Association estimates there are 27,000 local prosecutors in the United States today, spread throughout 2,341 jurisdictions. In many of these, especially the less populous ones, local prosecutors sometimes receive advice, guidance and even courtroom assistance from lawyers in the state attorney general's office. In three states—Delaware, Alaska and Rhode Island— the attorney general is the local prosecutor. When a conviction is appealed, the attorney general's office typically gets involved as a matter of course. So, it is common to hear defense lawyers praise or criticize assistant attorneys general much as they do district attorneys.

The top person in the office—elected in most jurisdictions, appointed in some—has a difficult job that becomes more difficult with each passing year. That is especially so in major metropolitan areas, where the top prosecutor must manage hundreds of lawyers and support staff, as well as deal with horrific crimes almost every day. The criminal justice system involves the complex interaction of all three branches of government (legislatures that write laws, executive branch officials—including prosecutors and police—who enforce them, and judges who interpret them). Further, crime rates vary from state to state and from city to city, or city to town. Comparisons of one jurisdiction with another are thus difficult to make.

For more than three years, the Center for Public Integrity studied the conduct of local prosecutors, trying to understand their actions within the context of a very difficult job. Center researchers analyzed every accessible state appellate court opinion, trial court ruling and state bar disciplinary filing back to 1970 addressing allegations of prosecutorial misconduct. Researchers supplemented these findings with additional cases not reported in court records but available through media accounts or learned of through interviews and correspondence with journalists, inmates, defense lawyers, state bar disciplinary counsel, judges and other sources.

The Center found the vast majority of opinions by searching the Lexis and Westlaw legal databases for the phrase "prosecutorial misconduct," a widely-used legal term that encompasses various bad acts by prosecutors, including withholding evidence, striking potential members of a jury on the bases of race or sex, or making improper opening or closing arguments. However, many cases involving acts that are arguably "prosecutorial misconduct" are not labeled or indexed as such by the court or the case law publishers. Generally, judges tend to limit the term to describe a particular kind of misconduct—namely, improper opening or closing arguments at trial. Thus, cases involving other acts that impinge on defendants' constitutional rights, such as Brady violations or subornation of perjury, were not discovered in the initial search.

Center researchers expanded their queries to find additional cases. They read the cases cited in the opinions located in the initial search. (The American legal system is based on precedent, so scattered throughout most opinions are citations to earlier cases that are used by the court to support their arguments and holdings.) The more thorough citation-check located dozens—sometimes even hundreds—of additional opinions per state for inclusion in our database.

Center researchers read 11,452 opinions dating from 1970. In 2,012 of them, appellate court judges reversed or remanded indictments, convictions or sentences due, in whole or in part, to prosecutorial misconduct. In 513 additional cases, appellate judges offered opinions—either dissents or concurrences—in which they found the prosecutorial misconduct serious enough to merit additional discussion; some of the dissenting judges wrote that they found the misconduct warranted a reversal. The reversals, remanded cases, and dissenting opinions have been entered into an online database. It is important to note that the findings of misconduct were made by appellate court judges, and not by Center researchers.

The Center's listing of mistrials and appellate reversals is by no means complete. While legal databases like Lexis and Westlaw contain appellate rulings, some remain unpublished—and thus would not be part of any legal database. And, short of visiting every courthouse in the country, there is no way to determine how many cases are dismissed or ruled mistrials by trial judges (thus never reaching the appellate courts) because of a prosecutor's misconduct.

In most of the opinions in the database, appellate judges do not name the prosecutor whose conduct—or misconduct—led to the reversal. When the prosecutor was not named, Center researchers contacted court clerks, district attorneys' offices, defense attorneys, and scanned local news sources to try to determine the name of the prosecutor in the case. To verify the information, researchers contacted the prosecutor directly. To determine the elected or appointed prosecutor in charge of the office at the time the misconduct occurred, researchers relied on public records.

As the cases in the Harmful Error database amply demonstrate, prosecutorial misconduct can happen at any stage of the criminal justice process—before, during and sometimes even long after the trial.

Misconduct and Punishment
State disciplinary authorities investigate prosecutors accused of misconduct

*U*nlike any private attorney, the local prosecutor—be he district attorney, county attorney, or criminal district attorney—is an elected official whose office is constitutionally mandated and protected. Prosecutors are still subject to the Rules of Professional Responsibility, but they must police themselves at the trial court level because of their status as independent members of the judicial branch of government. Such a holding is not tantamount to making the fox guardian of the henhouse or letting the wolf keep watch on the flock, because a prosecutor who violates ethical rules is subject to the disciplining authority of the State Bar like any other attorney. Perhaps even more importantly, as mentioned above, his violation of the rules will subject his cases to reversal on appeal when his unprofessional conduct results in a denial of due process to a defendant. Lastly, he, like all elected public officials, must regularly answer to the will of the electorate. Should his conduct create too much appearance of impropriety and public suspicion, he will ultimately answer to the voters.*—State ex rel. Eidson v. Edwards, 793 S.W.2d 1 (Tx. 1990)

Prosecutors, like other attorneys, must adhere to the standards of professional conduct that exist in the state where they practice. Every state has a disciplinary system under which lawyers can be punished for violating ethical standards. Some acts of prosecutorial misconduct, apart from leading to reversals of convictions, can constitute ethical violations and thus subject the prosecutor to disciplinary action by the state bar authority.

Discipline of any lawyer is a serious matter, because it can lead to the permanent loss of the lawyer's license to practice in the state. As with regular criminal defendants, therefore, lawyers entering the disciplinary system are afforded rights to ensure fair treatment. A thorough investigation of the case is conducted, and the lawyer is given the opportunity to present a defense. Disciplinary proceedings are normally kept confidential unless the bar authority or court imposes a public punishment. Funding for the disciplinary authority's operation usually comes from an annual fee assessed on all lawyers who practice in the state.

The process usually begins with the filing of a complaint at the bar disciplinary authority. For private attorneys, the complainant is normally a dissatisfied client. Since prosecutors do not have a "client" in the traditional sense, the complainant may be a defendant, defense lawyer or judge. After the complaint is filed, the disciplinary authority begins an inquiry. All complaints undergo a review process that might lead to the filing of formal charges against the lawyer, a trial-like formal hearing and, if warranted, the imposition of a punishment. Final decisions of the disciplinary authority can usually be appealed to the courts. In some states, the highest court is required to review all cases that result in suspension or disbarment.

Actual punishment of a lawyer can take several forms, depending on the particular circumstances, including the severity of the offense. Punishment in most states, however, follows the same basic progression in severity: private admonition or reprimand, public reprimand, suspension from the practice of law for a set period of time, and permanent disbarment from the practice of law. Additionally, the lawyer may also be assessed the cost of the disciplinary proceedings, which can run to thousands of dollars. In some cases, a period of probation with conditions the attorney must satisfy can be imposed in lieu of a more severe punishment. The disciplinary authority or court, at any stage of the process, may decide against imposing any sanction and dismiss the complaint.

The Center's Findings

The Center analyzed dozens of cases since 1970 in which local prosecutors appeared before state bar authorities for their misconduct.

Punishable misconduct by a prosecutor can take many forms. Prosecutors have faced discipline for committing crimes such as forgery and drug possession and, in jurisdictions where prosecutors are allowed to keep a private law practice on the side, for having conflicts of interest. In keeping with our study, however, we selected only those cases involving misconduct that affected the fundamental fairness of pending criminal proceedings or infringed on the constitutional rights of criminal defendants.

Examples of such misconduct include:

- discovery violations;

- improper contact with witnesses, defendants, judges or jurors;

- improper behavior during hearings or trials;

- prosecuting cases not supported by probable cause;

- harassing or threatening defendants, defendants' lawyers or witnesses;

- using improper, false or misleading evidence;

- displaying a lack of diligence or thoroughness in prosecution; and

- making improper public statements about a pending criminal matter.

Out of 44 attorney disciplinary opinions:

- In seven, the court dismissed the complaint or did not impose a punishment.

- In 20, the court imposed a public or private reprimand or censure.

- In 12, the prosecutor's license to practice law was suspended.

- In two, the prosecutor was disbarred.

- In one, a period of probation was imposed in lieu of a harsher punishment.

- In 24, the prosecutor was assessed the costs of the disciplinary proceedings.

- In three, the court remanded the case for further proceedings.

In two of the 44 cases, *In re Christoff* and *In re Conduct of Burrows*, two prosecutors were disciplined. The case of Hartford, Conn., prosecutor John Massameno was an action for declaratory relief that arose out of a pending state attorney grievance committee proceeding. Massameno argued that the disciplinary committee lacked the authority to punish him. The state high court disagreed and remanded the case to the committee, which subsequently cleared him of all wrongdoing in March 1997.

Of the 20 censures or reprimands, 19 are public. Appellate opinions that cite prosecutors for misconduct do not, for the most part, name the prosecutor who broke the rules. The Oklahoma Court of Criminal Appeal in the case of *Peninger v. State* offers a plausible explanation as to why courts are reluctant to name misbehaving prosecutors in their opinions: Publishing the name of a prosecutor (or any other kind of lawyer) is tantamount to issuing a public censure without affording the prosecutor the due process protections to which they are entitled in the attorney disciplinary system.

Suspensions in the cases found by the Center typically ranged from thirty days to six months. In the case of L. Gilbert Farr, the court imposed a suspension of six months on top of Farr's self-imposed two-year suspension. In the case of L. Forrest Price, the court imposed a five-year suspension, then stayed all but two years plus the time it would take him to comply with certain conditions. In the case of James Ramey, the court suspended him indefinitely with no possibility for reinstatement for three months.

Disbarment is the most serious professional penalty for an attorney. In the case of Kenneth Peasley, the full state disciplinary commission recommended disbarment in November 2002. Peasley appealed; his case is pending before the Arizona state Supreme Court. In the case of Thurston County, Wash., prosecuting attorney Charles O. Bonet, the Washington Supreme Court ruled in August 2001 that Bonet violated the state's attorney ethics rules and remanded the case to the disciplinary board to impose appropriate sanctions. On remand, the disciplinary board hearing officer recommended disbarment. Bonet was officially disbarred in April 2003.

In 24 cases, the prosecutors had to pay all or part of the cost of their hearings. The amounts that could be determined from the opinions ranged from $272.20 in the case of Linda J. Hansen to $12,156 in the case of Kenneth N. Johnson.

Disciplinary hearings often involve complex or novel legal issues. In the case of York County, Pa., district attorney Hugh Stanley Rebert, the Pennsylvania Supreme Court was asked to define the level of mental culpability necessary to prove whether Rebert's failure to disclose evidence to the defendant violated the ethics rules. The court did so and remanded the case to the disciplinary board for further proceedings. Rebert's disciplinary records, as of May 2003, show no public sanctions have ever been imposed against him.

Prosecutors who faced disciplinary committees because of their professional conduct

Prosecutor	Citation	Date	State and County of Practice	Misconduct	Disposition
Brian R. Barnes	574 P.2d 657	2/14/78	OR, Lane County	While prosecuting a rape case, Barnes sought a search warrant to obtain a blood sample from the defendant without notifying the court that a hearing on the matter was pending in another court.	Public reprimand
Francis W. Bloom	9 Mass. Attorney Discipline Reports 23	12/16/93	MA, Hampden County	Bloom authored a bogus confession in order to trick two suspects into confessing to a crime; the confession was later discovered in the file of the purported confessor by another prosecutor who planned to use it at trial until she discovered its falsity.	Public censure
Charles O. Bonet	29 P.3d 1242	8/23/01	WA, Thurston County	Bonet told a co-defendant witness that charges against him would not be prosecuted if he took the stand and pled the Fifth Amendment when called to testify for the other co-defendant.	Bonet violated the ethics rules; the case was remanded to the disciplinary board with directions for it to impose appropriate discipline. Bonet was officially disbarred in April 2003.
Allen R. Brey	490 N.W.2d 15	10/14/92	WI, Taylor County	Brey met with a criminal defendant he knew was represented by counsel without that counsel's knowledge or consent. Brey later denied to the court and the attorney disciplinary authority that the meeting had taken place.	Sixty-day suspension; costs

Prosecutor	Citation	Date	State and County of Practice	Misconduct	Disposition
Patrick J. Brophy	442 N.Y.S. 2d 818	9/17/81	NY, Richmond County	Brophy hid evidence and suborned perjury to convict organized crime figures. He was convicted of the misdemeanor of willfully depriving an individual of his rights and fined $500.	Public censure
Robert M. Burrows	618 P.2d 1283	11/4/80	OR, Josephine County	A defendant, who had confessed to murder, wrote a letter to his mother. The mother gave the letter, which made no specific reference to the murder, to Burrows and specifically authorized him to use it in any manner to help young people. While defendant's case was pending, Burrows read the letter to high school students.	Burrows' conduct did not violate the ethics rules; complaint dismissed.
Robert M. Burrows William D. Hostetler	629 P.2d 820	6/16/81	OR, Josephine County	District Attorney Burrows and Deputy District Attorney Hostetler communicated, and caused others to communicate, with a criminal defendant without obtaining his attorney's consent. Additionally, Burrows had *ex parte* communications with the judge regarding the defendant's case without notifying defendant's attorney, and Hostetler acted to conceal the communications with the defendant by failing to countermand police officers' suggestion to the defendant that he not tell his attorney.	Public reprimand; costs
Sue Carpenter	808 P.2d 1341	4/12/91	KS, Shawnee County	Carpenter's negligence in not diligently obtaining and reviewing medical reports deprived the defendant of a fair trial.	Public censure; costs

Prosecutor	Citation	Date	State and County of Practice	Misconduct	Disposition
Mark S. Christoff Richard M. Holmes	690 N.E.2d 1135	12/30/97	IN, Fountain County	Christoff threatened to renew a long-dormant criminal investigation against a political candidate seeking the office occupied by Holmes; Holmes filed a grievance with the disciplinary commission against the candidate.	Christoff: Public reprimand; costs Holmes: Thirty-day suspension; costs
Vance W. Curtis	656 N.E.2d 258	10/10/95	IN, Tipton County	Curtis represented a client when simultaneously, as a prosecutor, he was participating in an investigation of the client without consulting the client or the state about the dual representation.	Thirty-day suspension; costs
James H. Dumke	489 N.W.2d 919	10/14/92	WI, Rock County	Dumke committed several acts of misconduct in his capacity as both a private attorney and prosecutor. As a prosecutor, he communicated with a party he knew was represented by counsel without the counsel's consent.	Six-month suspension; costs
L. Gilbert Farr	557 A.2d 1373	5/26/89	NJ, Somerset County	Farr committed a series of gross improprieties after developing a personal relationship with two informants.	Six-month suspension (in addition to a self-imposed two-year suspension); costs
Daniel Peter Feinberg	760 So.2d 933	6/1/00	FL, Charlotte County	Feinberg continued to meet privately with opposing counsel's client despite knowing the client was represented by counsel; he affirmatively misled opposing counsel regarding those meetings.	Public reprimand; costs ($4,912.87)

Prosecutor	Citation	Date	State and County of Practice	Misconduct	Disposition
William E. Gerstenslager	543 N.E.2d 491	8/16/89	OH, Cuyahoga County	Gerstenslager failed to fully disclose exculpatory evidence in a rape case, conduct for which he was convicted of contempt of court and fined $500 plus costs.	Public reprimand; costs
Terese M. Gustafson	968 P.2d 367	11/13/98	OR, Clackamas County	Gustafson improperly threatened a defense lawyer handling a pending juvenile case with possible criminal and ethical charges and failed to disclose a material fact regarding those charges to the court.	Six-month suspension (In 2002, Gustafson was disbarred for failing to obey a court order and misleading the court regarding her handling of records in the juvenile matter.)
Bruce R. Hamilton	819 S.W.2d 726	12/19/91	KY, Henry County	During his prosecution of a criminal trial in 1984, Hamilton made a false statement of fact to the trial court regarding the destruction of evidence.	Fifty-nine day suspension; costs
Linda J. Hansen	877 P.2d 802	7/14/94	AZ, City of Phoenix	Hansen, an assistant city prosecutor, informed the court and defense counsel during a trial that the victim witness failed to appear, even though she had seen the witness at the courthouse earlier that day and told her she could leave.	Censure; costs ($272.20)
Charles H. Hatcher, Jr.	483 S.E.2d 810	2/21/97	WV, Cabell County	Allegedly, Hatcher knowingly failed to timely disclose exculpatory evidence to defense counsel during a criminal prosecution.	The attorney disciplinary board failed to prove the misconduct allegations by requisite clear and convincing evidence; disciplinary charges dismissed

Prosecutor	Citation	Date	State and County of Practice	Misconduct	Disposition
Cecelia G. Jarrell	523 S.E.2d 552	11/10/99	WV, Lincoln County	In one case, Jarrell conferred with a defendant without his counsel present. In another case, she falsely stated that there were no verbal plea offers; delayed the execution of a plea agreement until after a hearing where a defense lawyer sought the plea information, and failed to disclose an executed plea agreement to a co-defendant for more than three months.	Disciplinary charges dismissed due to "extraordinary mitigating circumstances"
Kenneth N. Johnson	477 N.W.2d 54	11/27/91	WI, Dodge County	Johnson failed to withdraw from prosecuting a case when the exercise of his professional judgment was affected by his own personal interest in preventing an investigation into the conduct of his office in the case.	Public reprimand; costs ($12,156)
Dwayne K. Jones	613 N.E.2d 178 (the facts of this case are more fully described in the Ohio attorney disciplinary board's findings issued on December 17, 1992)	6/16/93	OH, Summit County	At a domestic violence retrial, Jones failed to disclose to the court and defense counsel that he found exhibits defendant had used at the previous trial but later misplaced.	Six-month suspension; costs ($717.98)
William L. Lasswell	673 P2d 855	12/6/83	OR, Douglas County	Lasswell made public statements regarding suspects arrested during a drug raid before they were brought to trial.	Found not guilty of violating the ethics rules; complaint dismissed

Prosecutor	Citation	Date	State and County of Practice	Misconduct	Disposition
Julie Ann Leonhardt	930 P.2d 844	1/16/97	OR, Clatsop County	Leonhardt obtained an indictment without probable cause, altered the indictment after it had been signed by the grand jury and lied about the alterations to the court and others; in a separate incident, she improperly attempted to use her influence to alter the course of a criminal prosecution.	Disbarment
Steven M. Lucareli	611 N.W.2d 754	6/20/00	WI, Vilas County	Lucareli was alleged to have filed immediately before the start of a trial a criminal charge against the defendant's attorney that was not supported by probable cause.	The attorney disciplinary board failed to prove the misconduct allegations by requisite clear and satisfactory evidence; disciplinary proceeding dismissed
John M. Massameno	663 A.2d 317	8/1/1995	CT, Hartford	It was alleged that while prosecuting a sexual molestation case, Massameno interviewed the accused's wife, the complaining witness, in the absence of her attorney; prosecuted the case without probable cause to believe the accused was guilty; requested a psychiatric examination of the children victims to assess their testimonial capacity; and improperly cross-examined a defense witness.	Affirmed the judgment that held the state attorney grievance committee had jurisdiction to investigate and discipline Massameno for professional misconduct (In March 1997, the attorney grievance committee cleared him of all wrongdoing.)

Prosecutor	Citation	Date	State and County of Practice	Misconduct	Disposition
Robert T. Miller	677 N.E.2d 505	3/7/1997	IN, Monroe County	Miller assisted the cause of a civil plaintiff by prosecuting a concurrent criminal action against the civil defendant; during the pendency of the criminal action, Miller failed to comply with several discovery orders; after the criminal action was dismissed because of Miller's inaction, he resurrected the case after the statute of limitations expired.	Public reprimand; costs
R. Kathleen Morris	419 N.W.2d 70	11/13/87	MN, Scott County	Morris failed to disclose exculpatory evidence and violated a court order for sequestering a child witness.	Public reprimand; costs ($750.00)
Pamela F. Mucklow	35 P.3d 527	12/26/00	CO, Montezuma County	Case one: Mucklow failed to timely inform opposing counsel of a letter from a complaining witness recanting an allegation that the defendant had assaulted the witness. Case two: On the advice of the district attorney, she failed to timely inform opposing counsel of exculpatory information.	Public censure; costs
Mark C. Pautler	35 P.3d 571	4/2/01	CO, Jefferson County	Pautler knowingly and intentionally deceived a murder suspect into believing that he was a public defender during negotiations designed to encourage the suspect to surrender to the authorities; he failed to inform the suspect that he represented the state.	Three-month suspension; suspension stayed during a probationary period of 12 months; costs

Prosecutor	Citation	Date	State and County of Practice	Misconduct	Disposition
Kenneth J. Peasley	State Bar of Arizona Hearing Officer's Report and Recommendation, File No. 97-1909	7/1/02	AZ, Pima County	Peasley suborned perjured testimony at two murder trials.	Sixty-day suspension; one year probation; costs (In November 2002, the full disciplinary commission recommended disbarment; Peasley's case is pending before the state Supreme Court.)
L. Forrest Price	638 P.2d 1311	1/25/82	CA, San Diego County	Price altered evidence in a criminal trial and then attempted to cover up his actions.	Five-year suspension, stayed, with Price placed on probation for five years on condition that he be suspended for the first two years and such additional time as it took him to pass the state attorney ethics exam and that he comply with other conditions.
Joel I. Rachmiel	449 A.2d 505	8/4/82	NJ, Union County	Rachmiel prosecuted a defendant for murder. A writ of habeas corpus was granted after the conviction. Rachmiel, then in private practice, spoke out about the case before the prosecutor's office decided whether to retry the defendant.	Rachmiel's conduct did not violate the ethics rules; disciplinary charges dismissed. (In July 1978, while still a prosecutor, Rachmiel made public statements during ongoing grand jury deliberations. An ethics investigation was initiated but terminated after Rachmiel explained that he had been misquoted.)

Prosecutor	Citation	Date	State and County of Practice	Misconduct	Disposition
James W. Ramey	512 N.W.2d 569	2/23/94	IA, Polk County	During trial, Ramey made false statements regarding the authenticity of evidence; Ramey also failed to disclose exculpatory evidence in the same matter.	Suspended indefinitely, with no possibility for reinstatement for three months after the date of the court's opinion; costs
Beverly C. John Read	357 S.E.2d 544	6/12/87	VA, Rockbridge County	Read failed to disclose exculpatory eyewitness evidence.	Read did not violate his discovery obligations; the order of the Virginia State Bar Disciplinary Board that disbarred Read was reversed
Hugh Stanley Rebert	714 A.2d 402	7/8/98	PA, York County	In a rape/murder case, Rebert failed to give the defense a confession by the defendant and also failed to disclose his agreement with a jailhouse informant witness until after the witness testified.	Case remanded to the disciplinary board for further proceedings
Jeffrey Kim Roberts	503 S.E.2d 160	6/1/98	SC, Sixth Judicial Circuit	Roberts was convicted of requesting or agreeing to accept sexual favors from a female defendant in exchange for dismissing a charge of driving under the influence.	Disbarment
Roger Rook	556 P.2d 1351	11/18/76	OR, Clackamas County	Rook refused to plea bargain with 15 criminal defendants on the same basis as previously offered to another criminal defendant unless they dismissed their attorneys and employed other counsel.	Public reprimand
Frank Schaub	618 So.2d 202	5/13/93	FL, Manatee County	While prosecuting a murder trial, Schaub introduced irrelevant, improper and deliberately misleading evidence.	Thirty-day suspension; costs ($1,176.80)

Prosecutor	Citation	Date	State and County of Practice	Misconduct	Disposition
Marc A. Shafir	455 A.2d 1114	2/15/83	NJ, Essex County	Shafir placed the signature of his supervising attorney on plea forms without the supervisor's permission. He also misrepresented facts regarding an accused's case to a prosecutor in another county, potentially increasing the sentence.	Public reprimand; costs
William Raymond Sharpe	781 P.2d 659	10/30/89	CO, Jefferson County	While prosecuting a capital case, Sharpe made a racially insensitive remark regarding the accused in the presence of the accused's lawyer.	Public censure
George E. Westfall	808 S.W.2d 829	5/3/91	MO, St. Louis County	Westfall made public remarks disparaging a Missouri court of appeals judge who issued a ruling that favored a defendant he was prosecuting.	Public reprimand; costs
Robert D. Zapf	375 N.W.2d 654	11/5/85	WI, Kenosha County	Zapf sent a letter criticizing a defense lawyer to both the presiding judge and the lawyer's client without obtaining the lawyer's authorization; Zapf also failed to disclose discoverable evidence.	Public reprimand; costs
John C. Zimmermann	764 S.W.2d 757	1/23/89	TN, Davidson County	Zimmermann made statements to the media regarding pending criminal proceedings.	Private reprimand; costs (split with the attorney disciplinary board)
John C. Zimmermann	Notice of Public Censure in File No. 24039-5-CH	5/28/02	TN, Davidson County	In a murder case, Zimmermann misrepresented and withheld evidence.	Public censure

Actual Innocence
Exonerated defendants whose cases involved prosecutorial misconduct

The following tables summarize cases in which the innocence of defendants convicted of a crime has either been conclusively established or is supported by extremely credible and compelling evidence, and some sort of prosecutorial misbehavior or error occurred in the case.

The prosecutorial misconduct recounted here varies in terms of seriousness and the degree to which it caused or perpetuated the wrongful conviction or incarceration. In some cases, the misconduct alleged by a defendant or found by a court was not decisive in leading to a guilty verdict.

The first table lists cases in which a court cited prosecutorial misconduct in its opinions. The second lists cases in which defendants alleged misconduct, but appellate courts dismissed the claim or found the error was harmless.

Actual Innocence Cases in which Courts Found Prosecutorial Misconduct

Name	Randall Dale Adams
State/County	Texas — Dallas County
Case history	1977: convicted of capital murder and sentenced to death 1980: death sentence overturned; sentence commuted to life imprisonment 1988: key witness recanted his trial testimony and attested to Adams' innocence 1989: conviction overturned; Adams released from prison
Description of misconduct	In 1989, the Texas Court of Criminal Appeals overturned Adams' conviction, holding that prosecutor Douglas D. Mulder withheld a statement a witness gave to the police that cast doubt on her credibility and allowed her to give perjured testimony. Further, the court found that after Adams' attorney discovered the statement, Mulder falsely told the court that he did not know the witness' whereabouts.
Opinions in database	768 S.W.2d 281; 577 S.W.2d 717

Name	Kirk Bloodsworth
State/County	Maryland — Baltimore County
Case history	1985: convicted of first-degree murder, first-degree rape and first-degree sexual offense; sentenced to death 1986: conviction overturned because of a *Brady* violation 1987: reconvicted 1993: DNA exoneration; released from prison and pardoned
Description of misconduct	In 1986, the Maryland Court of Appeals overturned Bloodsworth's conviction because prosecutors Robert Lazzaro and Ann Brobst withheld evidence pertaining to another possible suspect.
Opinions in database	512 A.2d 1056

Name	Clarence Brandley
State/County	Texas — Montgomery County
Case history	1981: convicted of capital murder 1986: a witness tells authorities another man confessed to the crime 1989: conviction overturned 1990: released
Description of misconduct	In 1989, the Texas Court of Criminal Appeals overturned Brandley's conviction, finding that police and prosecutors, including James Keeshan, failed to investigate leads pertaining to other suspects, suppressed evidence placing other suspects at crime scene at time of crime, failed to call a witness who didn't support the state's case, allowed the perjured testimony of a witness to go uncorrected, and failed to notify Brandley that another man later confessed to the crime.
Opinions in database	781 S.W.2d 886; 691 S.W.2d 699

Name	Paris Carriger
State/County	Arizona — Maricopa County
Case history	1978: convicted of robbery and murder 1987 and 1991: state's key witness confessed to the crime 1997: conviction overturned 1999: released
Description of misconduct	In 1997, the United States Court of Appeals for the Ninth Circuit granted Carriger a new trial because the prosecutor, Richard Strohm, failed to disclose information that could have undermined the key witness' credibility.
Opinions in database	692 P.2d 991

Name	Kerry Max Cook
State/County	Texas — Smith County
Case history	1978: convicted of capital murder 1991: conviction overturned due to the erroneous admission of psychiatric testimony 1994: retried and convicted 1996: conviction overturned 1999: pled to a lesser charge; DNA exoneration
Description of misconduct	In 1996, the Texas Court of Criminal Appeals overturned Cook's conviction because the prosecutors, including A. D. Clark, Michael Thompson and David Dobbs, withheld and/or lied about evidence on a variety of matters concerning Cook's guilt and the credibility of state witnesses and attempted to interview Cook without the knowledge or consent of his lawyer. The court's opinion also notes that a state expert witness admitted that Clark pressured him to present false and misleading testimony.
Opinions in database	940 S.W.2d 623; 741 S.W.2d 928

Name	Rolando Cruz and Alejandro Hernandez
State/County	Illinois — DuPage County
Case history	1985: convicted of kidnapping, rape and murder; another man confessed 1988: convictions overturned 1990: Cruz reconvicted 1991: Hernandez reconvicted 1994: Cruz conviction overturned 1995: Hernandez conviction overturned; DNA exoneration; Cruz acquitted at third trial; charges against Hernandez dismissed 2000: Cruz, Hernandez and a third defendant prosecuted for the same crime won $3.5 million settlement from county
Description of misconduct	Cruz's first conviction was overturned because of prosecutor Thomas Knight's improper use of co-defendants' statements at trial. Cruz's second conviction was overturned in part because prosecutor Robert Kilander improperly impeached a witness. In 1996, prosecutors Knight, Kilander and Patrick King, along with four sheriff's detectives, were criminally charged with conspiring to convict Cruz and Hernandez by fabricating evidence and withholding exculpatory evidence. All were acquitted in 1999.
Opinions in database	521 N.E.2d 18; 1992 Ill. Lexis 221; 643 N.E.2d 636

Name	Henry Arthur Drake
State/County	Georgia — Madison County
Case history	1976: convicted of murder and armed robbery; sentenced to death on the murder charge 1981: state's key witness, the co-defendant, admitted he lied at Drake's trial and that he, not Drake, was responsible for the murder 1985: conviction overturned 1987: reconvicted; paroled later that year
Description of misconduct	In separate trials of Drake and the co-defendant, prosecutor Bryant Huff used two different theories as to who was the murderer. In 1985, the United States Court of Appeals for the Eleventh Circuit reversed Drake's death sentence because of Huff's improper remarks during the sentencing phase of trial.
Opinions in database	247 S.E.2d 57

Name	Ella Mae Ellison
State/County	Massachusetts — Suffolk County
Case history	1974: convicted of murder and armed robbery 1976: the two key witnesses recanted their trial testimony and claimed Ellison was innocent 1978: convictions overturned; released; all charges dropped
Description of misconduct	In 1978, the Supreme Judicial Court of Massachusetts overturned Ellison's convictions because the prosecutor withheld evidence that could have exonerated Ellison.
Opinions in database	379 N.E.2d 560

Name	Michael Ray Graham and Albert Ronnie Burrell
State/County	Louisiana — Union Parish
Case history	1987: convicted of first-degree murder and sentenced to death in separate trials 2000: charges dismissed; released
Description of misconduct	In granting a new trial for Graham in March 2000, a judge ruled that prosecutor Dan Grady had failed to disclose several pieces of exculpatory evidence. The judge also noted that Grady later provided an affidavit in which he admitted the case against Graham and Burrell was so weak it should not have been brought to the grand jury.
Opinions in database	561 So.2d 692 (Burrell)

Name	Ricky Hammond
State/County	Connecticut — Hartford-New Britain
Case history	1987: kidnapping and sexual assault; Hammond became a suspect
	1989: DNA and blood test exoneration
	1990: convicted
	1992: conviction overturned; new trial granted; was subsequently retried and acquitted
Description of misconduct	Despite pre-trial biological tests that exonerated Hammond, prosecutor John Malone at trial claimed the evidence had been contaminated, a claim the appellate court deemed highly improbable. However, the state at that time had other evidence that could have been — but was not — tested. The court also ruled that some of Malone's comments during closing argument were improper but not prejudicial enough to separately require reversal.
Opinions in database	604 A.2d 793

Name	Terry Harrington
State/County	Iowa — Pottawattamie County
Case history	1978: convicted of first-degree murder
	2000: "Brain Fingerprinting" test exoneration
	2003: conviction overturned; released
Description of misconduct	In overturning Harrington's conviction in 2003, the Iowa Supreme Court ruled that several police reports pointing to another suspect were not turned over and noted that a witness testified at a post-conviction hearing that he lied at Harrington's trial because police and prosecutors pressured him. In an earlier appeal, the court dismissed Harrington's claims that prosecutor Joseph Hrvol intimidated a defense witness, suborned the perjury of a state witness and committed improprieties in his dealings with other witnesses.
Opinions in database	284 N.W.2d 244; 659 N.W.2d 509

Name	J. L. Ivey, Jr.
State/County	New York — Erie County
Case history	1976: convicted of second-degree murder and first-degree robbery
	1981: conviction overturned
	1982: retried and acquitted; released
	1985: won a judgment against the state for wrongful conviction and imprisonment
Description of misconduct	The appellate court overturned Ivey's conviction because prosecutor Albert Ranni committed "numerous and repeated acts of improper and prejudicial conduct" at Ivey's trial, including attempting to offer into evidence misleading composite sketches in defiance of the court's rulings and making improper remarks to jury. In Ivey's wrongful conviction and imprisonment suit, the court found that Ivey had proven his innocence by clear and convincing evidence.
Opinions in database	443 N.Y.S.2d 452

Name	Lesly Jean
State/County	North Carolina — Onslow County
Case history	1982: convicted of first-degree sexual offense and first-degree rape
	1991: conviction overturned; charges dropped; released
	2001: DNA exoneration; pardoned; awarded compensation from state
Description of misconduct	In 1991, the United States Court of Appeals for the Fourth Circuit overturned Jean's conviction because the police and/or prosecutors failed to disclose evidence pertaining to the hypnosis of a key witness and the victim. Two judges dissented from the North Carolina Supreme Court's affirmance of Jean's conviction in 1984, finding that prosecutor Walter Vatcher's cross-examination of Jean was improper.
Opinions in database	311 S.E.2d 266

Name	Verneal Jimerson
State/County	Illinois — Cook County
Case history	1978: indicted on charges arising from a double murder; the charges were dis missed a month later because the key witness recanted her grand jury testimony
	1984: re-indicted on charges of murder
	1985: convicted
	1995: conviction overturned
	1996: DNA exoneration; another man confessed; Jimerson and three others convicted of the same crimes released from prison
	1999: The four receive $36 million from the state
Description of misconduct	In 1995, the Supreme Court of Illinois overturned Jimerson's convictions because the prosecutor, Scott Arthur, allowed the perjured testimony of the state's key witness to stand uncorrected.
Opinions in database	652 N.E.2d 278

Name	Ray Krone
State/County	Arizona — Maricopa County
Case history	1992: convicted of first-degree murder and kidnapping
	1995: conviction overturned
	1996: retried and convicted
	2002: DNA exoneration; released; charges dismissed
Description of misconduct	In 1995, the Arizona Supreme Court ordered a new trial because prosecutor Noel Levy did not turn over a crucial piece of evidence — a videotape an expert witness was preparing to use during his testimony — until the eve of trial.
Opinions in database	897 P.2d 621

Name	Steven Paul Linscott
State/County	Illinois — Cook County
Case history	1982: convicted of murder; acquitted of rape 1985: conviction overturned due to insufficient evidence 1986: conviction reinstated; case remanded 1987: conviction overturned due to prosecutorial misconduct 1991: case remanded for new trial 1992: DNA exoneration; charges dropped before retrial 2002: pardoned
Description of misconduct	The appellate courts overturned Linscott's conviction because the prosecutor made several misleading and improper statements regarding the forensic evidence.
Opinions in database	566 N.E.2d 1355

Name	Ronnie Marshall and Robert Spurlock
State/County	Tennessee — Sumner County
Case history	1990: convicted of first-degree murder at separate trials 1992: Marshall's conviction overturned 1993: Spurlock's conviction overturned 1995: Spurlock retried and convicted; Marshall plea bargained for a reduced sentence 1995-1996: the real killer confessed 1996: convictions vacated; released
Description of misconduct	The Tennessee Court of Criminal Appeals overturned Marshall's conviction because prosecutors Lawrence Ray Whitley and Jerry Kitchen failed to provide witness statements that pointed to other suspects A year later, the court overturned Spurlock's conviction because Whitley and Kitchen failed to provide exculpatory witness statements, failed to correct the false testimony given by prosecution witnesses and used false evidence.
Opinions in database	845 S.W.2d 228 (Marshall); 874 S.W.2d 602 (Spurlock)

Name	Walter McMillian
State/County	Alabama — Monroe County (tried in Baldwin County)
Case history	1988: convicted of capital murder and sentenced to death 1988-1992: all three witnesses recanted 1993: conviction overturned; released; charges dismissed
Description of misconduct	The Alabama Court of Criminal Appeals in 1993 ruled prosecutors did not disclose exculpatory evidence and reversed his conviction and death sentence.
Opinions in database	Not available

Name	Ruben Montalvo and Jose Morales
State/County	New York — Bronx County
Case history	1988: convicted of murder 2000: new evidence exoneration 2001: convictions vacated; released
Description of misconduct	A federal district court criticized the Bronx District Attorney's office's handling of the case. Leads pointing to other suspects, including repeated confessions by another man, were insufficiently investigated or ignored. Evidence that could have helped both men was either withheld or produced in redacted form. Trial prosecutor Allen Karen did not disclose the key witness' criminal history or correct her inaccurate testimony about drug use and improperly questioned a defense witness.
Opinions in database	Not available

Name	Charles Munsey
State/County	North Carolina — Wilkes County
Case history	1996: convicted of murder; another man confessed 1999: conviction overturned; new trial granted
Description of misconduct	In May 1999, the court ordered a new trial for Munsey because, among other errors, District Attorney Randy Lyon withheld evidence that would have cast doubt on the key witness' claim that Munsey confessed to him in prison.
Opinions in database	Not available

Name	Ellen Reasonover
State/County	Missouri — St. Louis County
Case history	1983: convicted of capital murder 1996: discovery of exculpatory evidence 1999: conviction overturned; released
Description of misconduct	Prosecutor Steven Goldman did not disclose exculpatory tape-recorded jail house conversations and other evidence that undercut the credibility of two key witnesses and failed to correct one witness' false testimony.
Opinions in database	714 S.W.2d 706

Name	James Joseph Richardson
State/County	Florida — Lee County
Case history	1968: convicted of murder 1988: someone else confessed 1989: released
Description of misconduct	In 1989, then-Dade County State's Attorney Janet Reno, appointed to re-investigate Richardson's case, concluded that the prosecutors and sheriff framed him by withholding exculpatory evidence, using perjured testimony and ignoring a suspect who later confessed she alone committed the crime.
Opinions in database	247 So.2d 296

Name	James E. Richardson, Jr.
State/County	West Virginia — Kanawha County
Case history	1989: convicted of rape, murder and arson 1996: conviction overturned 1998: DNA exoneration 1999: charges dropped; released
Description of misconduct	In September 1996, a Kanawha circuit judge overturned Richardson's conviction based on allegations that state police chemist Fred Zain fabricated evidence and that prosecutors withheld exculpatory evidence.
Opinions in database	Not available

Name	Edward Ryder
State/County	Pennsylvania — Philadelphia County
Case history	1974: convicted of first-degree murder and conspiracy 1991: discovery of new exculpatory evidence 1993: sentence commuted; paroled 1995: discovery of long-withheld exculpatory evidence 1996: conviction overturned
Description of misconduct	For more than twenty years, prosecutors withheld several exculpatory statements taken by police. Despite the emergence of evidence in 1991 casting considerable doubt on Ryder's guilt, the Philadelphia District Attorney's office refused to re-examine his case.
Opinions in database	31 Phila. 112

Name	Terry W. Seaton
State/County	New Mexico — Lea County
Case history	1973: convicted of first-degree murder 1979: released after new evidence cast strong doubt on his guilt 1981: awarded $150,000 in a wrongful arrest suit
Description of misconduct	On appeal, Seaton challenged several comments made by the two prosecutors at his trial. The court held that one comment was an "irresponsible" remark regarding Seaton's credibility and another misstated the evidence, but neither these nor the other challenged comments constituted prejudicial error. In 1979, a district court judge granted Seaton a new trial because the prosecution had suppressed evidence pointing to another suspect.
Opinions in database	525 P.2d 858

Name	Frank Lee Smith
State/County	Florida — Broward County
Case history	1985: convicted of first-degree murder, sexual battery and burglary with an assault 2000: died in prison; DNA exoneration later that year
Description of misconduct	In 1987, the Supreme Court of Florida ruled that the prosecution's submitting a new witness list on the day of trial did not constitute a discovery violation. The court also rejected Smith's claim that the prosecutor coached a witness outside the courtroom during the trial. In 1990, the court rejected Smith's claim that the prosecutor made inappropriate "victim impact" comments during trial but ordered a hearing to evaluate new evidence that a recanting witness might have been pressured by police and prosecutors to falsely implicate Smith. In 1998, after Smith was denied post-conviction relief, Smith appealed and the state Supreme Court remanded for another hearing because prosecutor Paul Zacks had engaged in improper *ex parte* communications with the judge presiding over the hearing while the judge was preparing his order. Smith was allowed to re-argue his new evidence claims, but the trial court once again denied relief.
Opinions in database	515 So.2d 182; 565 So.2d 1293; 708 So.2d 253

Name	Jerry Watkins
State/County	Indiana — Hancock County
Case history	1986: convicted of murder 1993: DNA exoneration 2000: conviction overturned; released
Description of misconduct	In 2000, a federal district court found that the prosecutor withheld exculpatory evidence.
Opinions in database	Not available

Name	Robert Wilkinson
State/County	Pennsylvania — Philadelphia County
Case history	1976: convicted of murder; released later in year after being exonerated by new evidence 1977: reindicted; indictments dismissed three months later
Description of misconduct	A federal court ruled prosecutor David Berman ignored, withheld and/or destroyed exculpatory evidence. In dismissing Wilkinson's later indictment, the court ruled the prosecution was being maintained in bad faith.
Opinions in database	Not available

Actual Innocence Cases in which Courts Rejected or Ruled as "Harmless Error" Allegations of Misconduct

Name	Mark Diaz Bravo
State/County	California — Los Angeles County
Case history	1990: convicted of rape 1990-93: victim recanted several times and named another man as her attacker 1993: DNA exoneration 1994: released
Description of misconduct	At trial, prosecutor Linda Chilstrom engaged in abrasive, discourteous and insulting conduct and misstated evidence, but the appellate court ruled it harmless error.
Opinions in database	18 Cal. App. 4th 1493

Name	Ronnie Bullock
State/County	Illinois — Cook County
Case history	1984: convicted of deviate sexual assault and aggravated kidnapping 1994: DNA exoneration; released; charges dropped
Description of misconduct	The prosecutor made improper closing arguments and withheld evidence regarding another suspected rapist, but the appellate court ruled both actions harmless error.
Opinions in database	507 N.E.2d 44

Name	Joseph Burrows
State/County	Illinois — Iroquois County
Case history	1988: murder/armed robbery 1989: convicted 1992-1994: two key witnesses recanted their trial testimony and one admitted she alone committed the crime 1994: won new trial; released 1996: charges dropped
Description of misconduct	The Supreme Court of Illinois upheld Burrows' conviction in 1992, rejecting his claims of pre-trial and trial prosecutorial misconduct. In 1996, the court affirmed the granting of a new trial for Burrows on the ground that two key witnesses recanted their testimony. The court noted that one of the witnesses testified at a post-conviction hearing he recanted a statement that might have helped Burrows because of prosecutor Tony Brasel's threats.
Opinions in database	592 N.E.2d 997

Name	Gary Dotson
State/County	Illinois — Cook County
Case history	1979: convicted of rape and aggravated kidnapping
	1985: victim admitted she fabricated rape claim; sentence commuted to time served
	1987: conviction affirmed
	1988: DNA exoneration
	1989: conviction overturned
Description of misconduct	The appellate court ruled that the prosecutor's conduct during Dotson's trial, which the trial judge censured at one point, was harmless error.
Opinions in database	424 N.E.2d 1319

Name	Michael Evans and Paul Terry
State/County	Illinois — Cook County
Case history	1977: tried jointly; convicted of murder, aggravated kidnapping, rape, deviate sexual assault, and indecent liberties with a child
	2001 & 2003: DNA exoneration
Description of misconduct	On direct appeal in 1979, the court ruled that some of the prosecutor's comments during closing argument were improper but harmless error. The court noted that Evans had previously been tried and convicted but was granted a new trial on the basis that the state had improperly withheld exculpatory evidence.
Opinions in database	399 N.E.2d 1333

Name	Charles I. Fain
State/County	Idaho — Canyon County
Case history	1983: convicted of first-degree murder, lewd and lascivious conduct with a minor and first-degree kidnapping
	2001: DNA exoneration; conviction overturned; charges dismissed; released
Description of misconduct	In 1989, the Supreme Court of Idaho affirmed his conviction, finding that the state's failure to preserve swabs of the victim's bodily fluid did not deprive him of a fair trial.
Opinions in database	Not available

Name	Anthony Michael Green
State/County	Ohio — Cuyahoga County
Case history	1988: convicted of rape and aggravated robbery
	2001: DNA exoneration; released
Description of misconduct	The appellate court, while recognizing that prosecutor Timothy McGinty made some "intemperate" comments during closing argument, nonetheless ruled them harmless error.
Opinions in database	585 N.E.2d 990

Name	Larry Holdren
State/County	West Virginia — Kanawha County
Case history	1984: convicted of sexual assault 1999: DNA exoneration; conviction overturned; released 2000: charges dismissed
Description of misconduct	In his federal habeas appeal, the court rejected his claim that the prosecutor committed misconduct at trial by eliciting improper testimony and making improper closing arguments.
Opinions in database	Not available

Name	Joe C. Jones
State/County	Kansas — Shawnee County
Case history	1986: convicted of aggravated kidnapping, rape and aggravated assault 1991: DNA exoneration 1992: conviction overturned; charges dismissed; released
Description of misconduct	In 1989, the Kansas Supreme Court ruled the prosecution's failure to turn over statements Jones made to the police did not deprive him of a fair trial.
Opinions in database	771 P.2d 73

Name	Ronald Jones
State/County	Illinois — Cook County
Case history	1989: convicted of murder and aggravated sexual assault 1997: DNA exoneration 1999: charges dropped
Description of misconduct	On appeal, Jones challenged comments the prosecutor made at trial. Although some of the prosecutor's comments were deemed slightly inaccurate and/or improper, the appellate court ruled them harmless error and affirmed the conviction.
Opinions in database	620 N.E.2d 325

Name	Kerry Kotler
State/County	New York — Suffolk County
Case history	1981: convicted of rape, robbery and burglary 1990: DNA exoneration 1992: conviction vacated; charges dismissed; released
Description of misconduct	Reviewing courts either dismissed or did not directly address Kotler's various claims of prosecutorial misconduct. In 1996, Kotler was arraigned on charges arising from a 1995 sexual assault. He was subsequently convicted.
Opinions in database	Not available

Name	Carlos Lavernia
State/County	Texas — Travis County
Case history	1985: convicted on charges of aggravated rape 2000: DNA exoneration; conviction overturned
Description of misconduct	In his federal habeas appeal, Lavernia alleged that during closing argument, the prosecutor impermissibly commented on his failure to testify. The court did not agree and denied habeas relief.
Opinions in database	Not available

Name	Larry Mayes
State/County	Indiana — Lake County
Case history	1982: convicted of rape, robbery and unlawful deviate conduct 2001: DNA exoneration; released
Description of misconduct	On appeal, Mayes unsuccessfully argued that the prosecutor made impermissible comments about his failure to testify.
Opinions in database	467 N.E.2d 1189

Name	James Newsome
State/County	Illinois — Cook County
Case history	1980: convicted of armed robbery, armed violence and murder 1994: new evidence exoneration; conviction overturned 1995: charges dropped; released; pardoned 1997: awarded $140,000 by state 2001: won $15 million in a civil suit against the Chicago police
Description of misconduct	In his 1982 appeal, the court rejected Newsome's claims that the prosecutor deprived him of a fair trial by excluding blacks from the jury and by misstating the evidence during rebuttal argument.
Opinions in database	Not available

Name	Marlon Passley
State/County	Massachusetts — Suffolk County
Case history	1996: convicted of murder and assault 1999: new evidence exoneration; released 2000: conviction overturned
Description of misconduct	The appellate court held that part of prosecutor Leslie O'Brien's closing argument, while not an entirely accurate recounting of the evidence, was not reversible error. The court also found no error in the way O'Brien examined defense witnesses.
Opinions in database	705 N.E.2d 269

Name	Jeffrey Todd Pierce
State/County	Oklahoma — Oklahoma County
Case history	1986: convicted of rape, burglary, sodomy and assault with a dangerous weapon 2001: DNA exoneration; released
Description of misconduct	On direct appeal in 1990, the Oklahoma Court of Criminal Appeals ruled that while the prosecutor made "unnecessary" comments at one point during trial, this did not amount to encouraging a state's witness to give improper testimony. The court also found that the forensic reports the state turned over before trial satisfied their discovery obligations. After he was exonerated, Pierce filed a civil suit claiming Oklahoma District Attorney Robert Macy conspired with police chemist Joyce Gilchrist to use false evidence to convict him.
Opinions in database	786 P.2d 1255

Name	Fredric Karl Saecker
State/County	Wisconsin — Buffalo County
Case history	1990: convicted of second-degree sexual assault, burglary and kidnapping 1995: new trial granted after DNA testing exonerated him 1996: charges dropped; released
Description of misconduct	In 1991, the Wisconsin Court of Appeals rejected Saecker's claim that the prosecutor failed to turn over exculpatory evidence.
Opinions in database	466 N.W.2d 911

Name	Yusef Salaam, Kevin Richardson, Antron McCray, Raymond Santana and Kharey Wise
State/County	New York — New York County
Case history	1989-1990: all were convicted on various counts, including rape, robbery and assault 1997: Salaam paroled 2002: another man confessed; DNA exoneration; all convictions vacated and indictments dismissed
Description of misconduct	In 1993, the New York Court of Appeals upheld Salaam's conviction; however, in a separate dissenting opinion, Judge Vito Titone criticized the way prosecutor Linda Fairstein kept Salaam's family and friends away while police questioned him. The crime for which the five were convicted is known as the "Central Park jogger attack."
Opinions in database	Not available

Name	Walter Smith
State/County	Ohio — Franklin County
Case history	1986: convicted of rape, kidnapping, aggravated burglary and robbery 1996: DNA exoneration; released 2001: awarded nearly $250,000 for wrongful imprisonment
Description of m isconduct	In 1988, the Ohio Court of Appeals rejected Smith's claims that the prosecutor withheld exculpatory evidence, improperly cross-examined him, and made prejudicial comments in closing argument
Opinions in database	1988 Ohio App. Lexis 3032

Name	Steven L. Toney
State/County	Missouri — St. Louis County
Case history	1982: convicted of forcible rape and sodomy 1996: DNA exoneration; released
Description of misconduct	In 1984, the Missouri Court of Appeals rejected Toney's claims that the prosecutor made an improper statement while examining a witness, impermissibly amended the charging document and did not properly disclose a state rebuttal witness. In 1996, a federal appeals court ruled that the prosecutor's use of a surprise rebuttal witness was not a violation of Toney's rights.
Opinions in database	Not available

Name	Nathaniel Walker
State/County	New Jersey — Union County
Case history	1976: convicted of kidnapping, rape and sodomy 1986: new evidence exoneration; charges dismissed; released
Description of misconduct	On direct appeal, the New Jersey appellate courts reversed — but later reinstated — his conviction on the issue of whether prosecutor Richard Rodbart made impermissible comments to the jury about Walker's failure to call an alibi witness.
Opinions in database	403 A.2d 1

Name	Terry Lee Wanzer
State/County	Georgia — Clayton County
Case history	1973: convicted of rape and aggravated sodomy 1981: paroled 1991: pardoned 1996: awarded $100,000 by the state
Description of misconduct	On appeal in 1974, the Georgia Supreme Court rejected Wanzer's claims that he was deprived of a fair trial when the prosecutor, through the bailiff, made an unauthorized communication with the jury during their deliberations and questioned a defense witness about perjury. The court also ruled the prosecutor did not withhold exculpatory evidence.
Opinions in database	207 S.E.2d 466

Name	Collin Warner
State/County	New York — Kings County
Case history	1982: convicted of second-degree murder 2001: co-defendant confessed he acted alone; conviction vacated; released
Description of misconduct	An appellate court in 1986 found that the prosecutor's comments during closing argument did not prejudice Warner.
Opinions in database	501 N.Y.S.2d 889

Name	Calvin Washington
State/County	Texas - McLennan County
Case history	1987: convicted of capital murder 2000-2001: DNA exoneration 2001: released and pardoned
Description of misconduct	Although agreeing the prosecutor made improper comments at trial, the Texas Court of Appeals rejected Washington's claim that these comments deprived him of a fair trial. The court also rejected Washington's claim that the prosecutor failed to disclose exculpatory evidence.
Opinions in database	822 S.W.2d 110 (Washington)

Name	Kenneth Waters
State/County	Massachusetts — Middlesex County
Case history	1983: convicted of first-degree murder and armed robbery 2001: DNA exoneration; released
Description of misconduct	On direct appeal in 1987, the court rejected Waters' claim that the state withheld exculpatory evidence.
Opinions in database	506 N.E.2d 859

Name	Johnny Lee Wilson
State/County	Missouri — Jasper County
Case history	1987: convicted of first-degree murder 1988: another man confessed 1995: released; pardoned
Description of misconduct	In 1990, the Missouri Court of Appeals declined to provide post-conviction relief on Wilson's claim that prosecutor Scott Sifferman withheld evidence that another suspect committed the murder.
Opinions in database	1990 Mo. App. Lexis 1663

State-by-State List of Cases Reviewed by the Center

• *Number of opinions reviewed by the Center in which defendants allege prosecutorial misconduct:* **11,452**

• *Number of opinions in which indictments, convictions or sentences were reversed due to prosecutorial misconduct:* **2,012**

• *Number of opinions in which the court ruled the misconduct harmless error:* **8,709**

• *Number of opinions in which the court did not address the misconduct allegations:* **731**

• *Number of opinions in which a concurring or dissenting judge filed a separate opinion criticizing the prosecutorial misconduct:* **513** *(In 468, the judge voted to reverse; in 45, the judge expressed displeasure with the prosecutor's behavior but didn't believe reversal was warranted).*

State	Opinions	Reversals	Harmless Error	Not Addressed	Dissent/ Concurrence
Alabama	325	69	223	33	5
Alaska	74	17	52	5	1
Arizona	302	39	254	9	8
Arkansas	54	7	38	9	4
California	590	75	461	54	41
Colorado	166	21	134	11	7
Connecticut	325	24	270	31	12
Delaware	151	22	102	27	0
Florida	569	253	281	35	19
Georgia	449	39	373	37	17
Hawaii	80	17	60	3	1
Idaho	102	8	86	8	10
Illinois	630	158	431	41	27
Indiana	475	21	423	31	12
Iowa	110	10	90	10	5
Kansas	231	31	197	3	1
Kentucky	121	37	81	3	9
Louisiana	168	27	134	7	15
Maine	94	17	75	2	0
Maryland	103	23	76	4	5
Massachusetts	189	31	152	6	5
Michigan	212	37	163	12	14
Minnesota	240	32	186	22	6

State	Opinions	Reversals	Harmless Error	Not Addressed	Dissent/ Concurrence
Mississippi	167	26	130	11	17
Missouri	376	77	288	11	21
Montana	69	8	53	8	4
Nebraska	72	6	57	9	2
Nevada	162	23	135	4	10
New Hampshire	29	3	25	1	1
New Jersey	178	42	122	14	15
New Mexico	133	19	107	7	3
New York	1283	277	906	100	45
North Carolina	120	14	104	2	7
North Dakota	26	5	20	1	1
Ohio	441	71	354	16	17
Oklahoma	308	30	271	7	16
Oregon	44	8	34	2	2
Pennsylvania	523	67	392	64	36
Rhode Island	49	4	43	2	2
South Carolina	61	19	40	2	5
South Dakota	54	3	47	4	13
Tennessee	200	18	172	10	2
Texas	589	154	420	15	42
Utah	115	13	98	4	2
Vermont	58	12	39	7	1
Virginia	127	22	101	4	8
Washington	244	18	217	9	2
West Virginia	59	20	36	3	2
Wisconsin	107	29	71	7	1
Wyoming	98	9	85	4	12
TOTAL	**11452**	**2012**	**8709**	**731**	**513**

A District Attorney Responds

July 7, 2003

Dear Center for Public Integrity:

The study entitled "Harmful Error" claims that prosecutorial misconduct is epidemic among the thousands of state and county prosecutors. The truth is that such misconduct is better described as episodic, those few cases being rare enough to merit considerable attention by both the courts and the media.

There is no question that given the critical role of gatekeeper the district attorney holds in our legal system the men and women who work as prosecutors should continue to be held to the highest standards of conduct. In the criminal justice system there is an elaborate system of checks and balances designed to protect both the innocent and the guilty. Alone among the legal profession, a prosecutor's sole allegiance is to the truth - even if that means torpedoing the prosecutor's own case.

When trial judges make mistakes appellate courts will reverse or remand those cases. We call these cases "judicial error." When defense attorneys fail to properly represent their clients, the accused's conviction is frequently set aside because of "inadequate assistance of counsel." Yet when a prosecutor makes an error it's called "prosecutorial misconduct," a term that summons up images of a district attorney hiding evidence, lying to a jury, or framing an innocent suspect. The reality is that overwhelming majority of prosecutorial errors are indeed "harmless" not "harmful," meaning that there was no malice on the part of the D.A. and that there was no unjust result. Keep in mind that only the defense has the right to appeal misconduct and therefore there is no judicial review of misconduct by a defense attorney.

How pervasive are instances of true misconduct by prosecutors? Because record keeping varies so much from one state to another it would be unwise to draw any sweeping conclusions across the country. The statistics on this website about my own state of Oregon show that in the last 33 years Oregon's appellate courts have raised issues of prosecutorial error 44 times but in only eight of those instances the prosecutors conduct was found to be prejudicial. Comparing those numbers against the thousands of criminal appeals rendered during this same time provides a rate of prosecutorial misconduct of less than one tenth of one percent. It is even more instructive to look at what kind of misconduct was deemed "prejudicial"—in one of those eight cases it was the exasperated description of a professional defense witness in a drunk driving case as a "pimp." The prosecutor never should have made the comment, but it is hardly in the same class as concealing evidence.

The study implies that in those rare cases where prosecutors get caught, little more than a slap on the wrist is given. The researchers missed no less than two cases in the past ten years in Oregon where elected prosecutors were permanently disbarred for misconduct in office. I should know—I have been three times elected District Attorney of Clatsop County where I was originally appointed by the governor to replace the previous District Attorney who was indicted, convicted, jailed and disbarred.

Prosecutors continue to be subject to the harshest sanctions on those truly rare occasions where they violate their oaths. No human endeavor is error free and the only way to achieve even lower error rates is simply to avoid prosecutions altogether.

Joshua Marquis is past president of the Oregon District Attorneys Association and a member of the board of directors of the National District Attorneys Association. He has practiced law for more than 20 years in several Oregon counties.

[**Editors' Note**: The Center thanks District Attorney Joshua Marquis for his thoughtful response. We agree that prosecutorial misconduct is episodic, not epidemic. We never said—or meant to imply—otherwise. We also thank Mr. Marquis for pointing out that we did not cite two cases in Oregon of elected prosecutors who were permanently disbarred for misconduct in office. We have made the corrections in our database and posted them on our website.]